The Great Minneapolis Line

CATALOGUE 1910

Home Office and Factory, Covering 80 Acres.

The Minneapolis Threshing Machine Co.

WEST MINNEAPOLIS, & HOPKINS P.O. MINN.

MINNEAPOLIS-MOLINE
TRACTORS 1870–1969

Text by C.H. Wendel & Photography by Andrew Morland

Motorbooks International
Publishers & Wholesalers

Acknowledgments

Thanks to all the owners of Minneapolis-Molines who allowed me to photograph their classic tractors. Thanks especially to Roger Mohr and his family, who kindly arranged his Minneapolis-Moline collection for photographs.

Anyone who is interested in Minneapolis-Moline tractors should contact *The MM Corresponder*, RT1 Box 153, Vail, IA 51465 USA.

First published in 1990 by Motorbooks International Publishers & Wholesalers, P O Box 2, 729 Prospect Avenue, Osceola, WI 54020 USA

© C. H. Wendel, text; Andrew Morland, photographs, 1990
Reprinted 1997

Motorbooks International books are also available at discounts in bulk quantity for industrial or sales-promotional use. For details write to Special Sales Manager at the Publisher's address

Library of Congress Cataloging-in-Publication Data
Wendel, C. H. (Charles H.)
    Minneapolis-Moline tractors, 1870–1969
/ C.H. Wendel, Andrew   Morland.
      p. cm.
    ISBN 0-87938-468-9
    1. Minneapolis-Moline tractors—
History. I. Morland, Andrew.
II. Title.
TL233.5.W46 1990   90-35074
631.3'72—dc20   CIP

Printed in Hong Kong

On the front cover: *A Minneapolis-Moline Universal ZB tractor factory-fitted to run on LP gas. The engine produced 32 hp at 1500 rpm and used a five-speed gearbox. The ZB was constructed from 1953 to 1955.*

On the back cover: *The Minneapolis-Moline Five Star of 1957, from the Roger Mohr Collection. An R model complete with enclosed cab rests in the background.*

On the frontispiece: *The grand artwork from the cover of the 1910 Minneapolis Threshing Machine Co. brochure shows the factory in Hopkins, Minnesota. Presumably, the farmer was allowed to rest because the mechanized machines were doing the brunt of the work.*

On the title page: *The Minneapolis-Moline RTE of 1949, from the Roger Mohr Collection. This RTE had an extendible front axle and pulls a Minneapolis-Moline LS manure spreader.*

Contents

Introduction

To condense the history of Minneapolis-Moline and its predecessor companies into a single volume is to condense some major events in the history of mechanized agriculture. A 1929 merger formed the new Minneapolis-Moline Power Implement Company. The three companies involved were Moline Plow Company, Minneapolis Steel & Machinery Company and Minneapolis Threshing Machine Company. Each in its own way had contributed mightily to mechanized farming. Each firm had its own distinctive way of doing business, and for various reasons, each firm had had its share of financial woes. In the end, the thought of a merger was not only desirable, it was also imperative.

This book is not intended as a comprehensive, in-depth study of

Front end of the Twin City MTA: power, muscle and poise.

Minneapolis-Moline (M-M) and its predecessors. Rather, it is based primarily on photographs of tractors now restored and preserved for posterity. Also included are illustrations from various advertising pieces dating back to the early 1900s. Tractors are the main emphasis, to the virtual exclusion of an extensive implement line. The M-M tractor line is well represented, but again the offering was so extensive, especially in later years, that the major portion is displayed but does not include each and every model. It should also be noted that on some of the constantly changing models, modifications were primarily cosmetic; with some new tinwork, new decals and a different color layout, a given tractor model got new clothes but still had the same body.

Initially, the tractor line consisted of Twin City tractors from Minneapolis Steel & Machinery Co. In a short time,

these were called M-M Twin City tractors, and by the late 1930s the Twin City name was dropped entirely. The tractors from Minneapolis Threshing Machine were phased out, probably after using up the remaining parts inventory. The Minneapolis grain threshers remained, however, as did the corn shellers and a few other machines. It would be logical to assume that these remaining Minneapolis machines probably formed the basis for later M-M machinery, including combines and the popular Model E corn sheller.

Moline Plow Co. had been in the tractor business for a few years with its Moline Universal, but after it left the market in 1923, Moline Plow stayed out of the tractor business, concentrating instead on its established implement lines.

Thus, each member of the M-M trilogy had unique features which when combined gave the new organization the rank of a full-line company. The powerful

This Farm
MINNEAPOLIS
TRACTOR
Built by MINNEAPOLIS-MOLINE

competition from John Deere, Case and International Harvester made this imperative. The emergence of Allis-Chalmers in the 1930s as a formidable opponent likewise fueled competitive fires. For this, if for no other reason, the three companies of this triad were forced to make the choice to merge or quit. They chose to merge in 1929, remaining in business under the Minneapolis-Moline name until merging with Oliver Farm Equipment Corporation and Cockshutt Farm Equipment Company to form White Farm Equipment Company in 1969.

Throughout the book I frequently cite the Nebraska Tractor Tests. In 1985 I wrote a book entitled *Nebraska Tractor Tests Since 1920* for Crestline Publishing which illustrates and describes every tractor tested at Lincoln, Nebraska. The book may be helpful in providing further information on M-M tractors, as well as giving data on those models not shown in this book.

This metal sign stating "This Farm is Minneapolis-Moline Tractor Operated" was intended for the gatepost of every M-M tractor owner. Although this 1950s advertising gimmick probably did little to overtly enhance new tractor sales, it undoubtedly kept the M-M name in people's minds.

9

ECONOMY

All Steel and Iron Except the Pole.

Disc

Steel Truss Frame.

Harrow

Made by

MOLINE PLOW COMPANY

MOLINE, ILL.

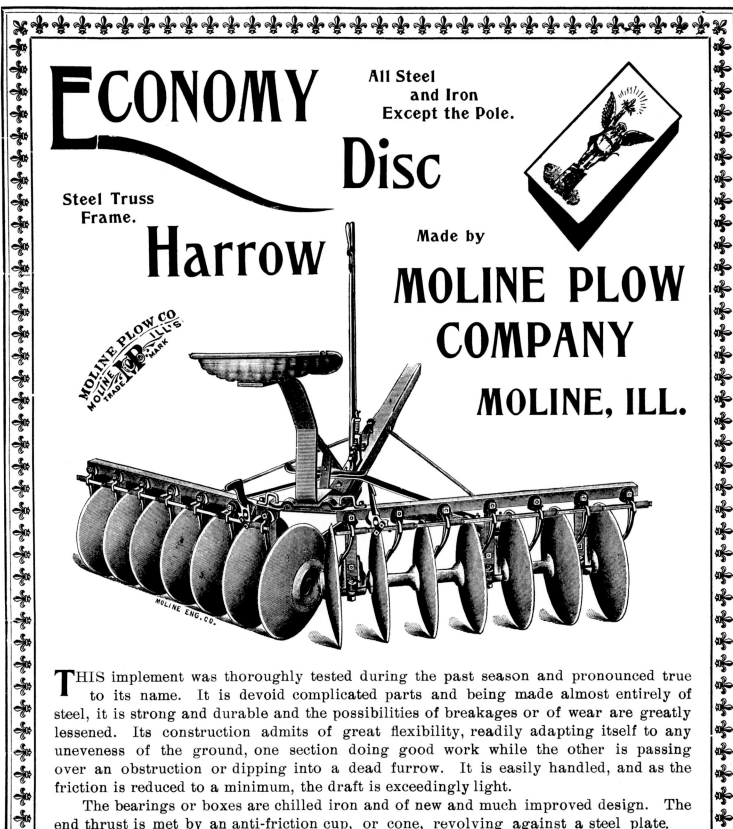

THIS implement was thoroughly tested during the past season and pronounced true to its name. It is devoid complicated parts and being made almost entirely of steel, it is strong and durable and the possibilities of breakages or of wear are greatly lessened. Its construction admits of great flexibility, readily adapting itself to any unevenness of the ground, one section doing good work while the other is passing over an obstruction or dipping into a dead furrow. It is easily handled, and as the friction is reduced to a minimum, the draft is exceedingly light.

The bearings or boxes are chilled iron and of new and much improved design. The end thrust is met by an anti-friction cup, or cone, revolving against a steel plate.

Moline Plow Company 1870–1929

Plowing Over the New American Frontiers

Organized in 1870, Moline Plow Co. had roots going back to 1852. At that time, the partnership of Candee & Swan began building hay rakes, chain pumps and other implements. Its location at Moline, Illinois, was advantageous because of excellent local markets and shipping facilities.

In about 1865 the partners entered the plow business, enticing an excellent plow maker into the company by making him a partner. During the next twenty years

A turn-of-the-century advertisement illustrates the Economy Disc Harrow from Moline Plow Co. As can be seen in this illustration, the Flying Dutchman line used a distinctive trademark with a short, fat Dutchman standing on a stump and holding up an ear of corn for all the world to see. It is said that the trademark was abandoned with the outbreak of World War I and its associated anti-German sentiments.

Moline Plow concentrated its sales efforts on the new American frontiers of Kansas, Minnesota and the Dakotas. Wherever there was a new influx of settlers, there was Moline Plow Co. This aggressive pursuit of the market brought the company into prominence.

Early mergers

In 1883 the company acquired rights for the G. W. Hunt patent, covering a new sulky plow design. Called the Flying Dutchman, it soon became popular and was in fact the mainstay of the Moline line for some years. By the 1890s Moline Plow Co. was a major exporter of plows and other implements. The Flying Dutchman plow was shipped to Denmark in large numbers and was christened there as the Danish Dutchman.

W. E. Waterman's check-row corn planter was added to the line in 1884, and soon the Champion planters were to be found all over

America. Cultivators got their impetus from the designs of August Lindgren as his first design was acquired by Moline in 1886. Over the next decades, Lindgren acquired a great many patents for Moline Plow Co., including his 1887 patent for a combination plow and planter, not at all unlike today's lister.

Moline Plow began to establish branch houses in the 1890s to improve distribution. It also took an aggressive look at overseas trade, finally securing a greater portion through the purchase of Adriance, Platt & Company. In this case, Moline was interested in Adriance because of its already established sales organization in the European countries. Acquisition of Adriance, Platt was therefore a sure method of increasing Moline's share of this market. Beyond this, Adriance already had a large market share in the northeastern states and was well accepted in this area. These

PLOWING   HARROWING   PLANTING   SEEDING   CULTIVATING   MOWING

Regularly Equipped
With Self Starter
and Electric Lights

MOLINE UNIVERSAL TRACTOR

MOLINE

MOLINE ACME STEEL WARRANTED

MOLINE ACME STEEL WARRANTED

Here are a Few of the Features that Make the Moline-

1. Does as much work with two bottoms as the ordinary three-plow tractor, due to its higher speed, 3 1-2 miles an hour.
2. 98 per cent of weight on drive wheels. No dead weight to push along. All weight goes into pull.
3. High clearance, 29 1-2 inches, and light weight, 3380 pounds, make tractor ideal for cultivating.
4. Universal adaptability for all farm operations—plowing, discing, planting, mowing, harvesting, etc., etc.
5. One man controls both tractor and implement from seat of implement, where he must sit to do good work.
6. Tractor backs with implement as readily as it goes forward, due to implement forming a single unit with it.

7. Easier to control and steer than any other tractor. A wom or boy handles it with ease. Turns in 16-foot circle.
8. Land wheel is instantly lowered for plowing, so that tract runs level when right wheel is in the furrow.
9. Electrical governor permits instant fixing of engine-speed any desired number of r. p. m.
10. Self starter avoids back breaking labor and saves time field—also fuel.
11. Electric lights illuminating both tractor and implement enab crowding of work in rush season.
12. Perfected overhead-valve four-cylinder engine gives smoo even flow of power—easy on bearings.

RAKING HAY | HARVESTING GRAIN | HARVESTING CORN | ODD JOBS | SPPF | BELT WORK

sal Tractor Model D Supreme in the Farm Tractor Field:

3. Engine lubrication under 35 pounds pressure causes bearings to float on film of oil.

4. Short, heavy crankshaft 2 1-2 inches in diameter and light reciprocating parts eliminate vibration.

5. Overhead-valve construction of engine and small bore, 3 1-2 inches, insure extreme operating economy.

6. Double valve springs give quick action with soft seating, prolonging life of valves materially.

7. Offset fulcrum of rocker arms enables use of light valve springs and reduces lift of cams by one half.

8. Every working part of the tractor, from fan bearing to final drive, completely enclosed in dust proof housings.

19. Tractor has no frame. Parts bolted directly together, insuring permanent alignment of shafts and bearings.

20. Transmission gears drop forged, cut and hardened. Seven splined shafts facilitate take down of transmission.

21. Fifteen Hyatt heavy duty roller bearings and five high grade ball thrust bearings used in tractor altogether.

22. Differential lock doubles pulling power of drive wheels in soft ground.

23. Internal expanding brakes on differential shafts hold tractor under perfect control under all conditions.

24. Complete provision for inspection and adjustment throughout tractor. Valves can be easily and accurately adjusted.

13

Moline-Mandt Wagon

Previous page
Moline Plow Co. could trace its roots all the way back to 1852. By the turn of the century the Moline implement line was known worldwide. In the latter part of 1915 Moline entered the tractor business, offering this Model D Universal from 1918 to 1923. The Universal was probably the first tractor to have a complete line of implements designed especially for its unique hitch system. After the Universal went out of production, Moline concentrated its efforts once again on implements, never again entering the tractor market.

factors were certainly no disadvantage to Moline.

By the turn of the century the Stephens family held a controlling interest in Moline Plow Co., retaining control until John N. Willys bought eighty-two percent of the common stock in 1918. Under the Stephens leadership, Moline began an aggressive plan of plant acquisitions to bolster and enhance existing product lines. Recalling that the early years of the twentieth century were filled with mergers and rumors of more, it is entirely possible that companies like Moline were panic-driven to some extent.

One of the first major

In addition to an extensive line of plows, cultivators and other implements, Moline Plow was well known for its line of wagons. In 1906 the company acquired the T. G. Mandt Co. of Stoughton, Wisconsin. This put the company squarely into the wagon business with a line that was already well established and with the highest reputation. A Moline-Mandt wagon of 1919 is shown from a company catalog.

purchases was the Acme Steel Company of Chicago. Prior to this purchase, Moline Plow Co. had been buying plow shares from the

Moline Wide Spread Spreader No. 50

A 1918 Moline Plow catalog illustrates the Moline Wide Spread Spreader Number 50. Until the early 1900s, farmers were forced to load manure into a wagon or whatever was handy, haul it to the field and then scatter it with forks. Thus, the manure spreader aided materially in reducing the labor-intensive farming methods of the time. The great demand for spreaders made them easy to sell for several years, and this attractive unit with a red body and yellow trim was no exception.

J. I. Case Plow Works and a few other companies. A buyout of Acme Steel meant that Moline could now manufacture its own plow shares, cultivator shovels and other steel items. This 1904 acquisition was in addition to the purchase of the T. G. Mandt Vehicle Company at Stoughton, Wisconsin. Mandt had been in the wagon business for many years and had built a sterling reputation in his field. Thus, the addition of Moline-Mandt wagons provided additional revenue, and the brightly painted

red and green Moline-Mandt wagons in almost every neighborhood didn't hurt the public image, either.

During 1906 the Stephens family bought out the Henney Buggy Company and the Freeport Carriage Company, both at Freeport, Illinois. Again, these were firms of the highest reputation; they had an already established clientele and they had the manufacturing capacity for large-scale production. In fact, during 1910 the Henney factory built about 30,000 buggies, and Freeport Carriage Company produced nearly 20,000. Within a few years, however, these plants were one of several millstones about the neck of Moline Plow Co.

To further enhance the farm implement line, Moline Plow had been marketing grain drills for several years, finally buying out the Monitor Drill Company of St. Louis Park, Minnesota, in 1909. In retrospect, this purchase was a wise one; in fact, the Monitor plant was one of the last vestiges of company assets by 1925.

Farmers of the early 1900s often had a farm scale. Usually, it was a platform scale large enough for a wagon. At this point in time there was a considerable demand, so in 1911 Moline bought out the McDonald Bros. Scale Company of Pleasant Hill, Missouri. Immediately the plant and McDonald were moved to the Stoughton, Wisconsin, factory.

I have never been sure of why or how John N. Willys was so intensely interested in acquiring Moline Plow, but from all appearances he had become a large stockholder as early as 1914. The Moline Automobile Company had begun building cars in 1904, continuing with rather modest styles until 1913. Since Moline Automobile and Moline Plow were both controlled by the Stephens family, the two companies were, in effect, one and the same.

In 1914 the Moline-Knight automobile first appeared and became standard the following year. Edwards Motor Company of New York had introduced its Edwards-Knight in 1912, and when

POWER ON PARADE
"Aces of Action"

Preferred Power Without A Premium In Price

M-M TWIN CITY TRACTORS are the pioneers of Modern Tractor design, backed by more than two decades of success. TWIN CITY was one of the first two really engineered lines of tractors to appear on the American market, and today, as always, M-M tractors are the standard of quality and economical power. "Balanced weight and power!" — MOST MODERN ENGINEERING! — M-M TWIN CITY Tractor owners are always assured of ample power at lowest cost and extra years of economical operation. 6 Modern Models.

Also makers of the complete line of MOLINE "FLYING DUTCHMAN" IMPLEMENTS, MOLINE-MONITOR DRILLS, MINNEAPOLIS THRESHERS, CORN SHELLERS, The HARVESTOR, *Modern Economy Combine,* and HAMMER MILLS.

Orchard "J"

Standard "J"

Universal "J"

Universal "M"

The "KT-A"

The "FT-A"

THE MODERN TRACTOR LINE

it fell into financial straits, the already successful Willys took over the company. With this buyout came the Willys-Knight, another car using the double-sleeve-valve engine. Yet another sleeve-valve machine was the Stearns-Knight, also appearing in 1914. Stearns would end up in the Willys portfolio in 1925.

None of the Knight sleeve-valve engines were a raging success. Despite certain advantages, the sleeve-valve engines were expensive to build and virtually impossible to maintain by the average shade-tree mechanic. By comparison, a good many Ford Model T engines were overhauled over a couple of sawhorses or on the kitchen table.

Despite rather poor auto sales, and despite advice to the contrary, Moline seemed resolute on staying in the automobile business. This great optimism even went so far as to announce a new one-and-one-half-ton truck in June 1920

The Moline Universal tractor

On the farm tractor scene, Moline Plow Co. definitely had a desire to break into the blooming tractor market. In 1913 a newly designed motor plow was presented to the Board of Directors, and they approved the building of five prototypes. These were then built for Moline by International Harvester Company, but by November of 1913 the idea was scrapped.

From the mid 1930s comes this advertisement showing the M-M Twin City line of that time. At this point M-M retained the Flying Dutchman trade name of Moline Plow Co., the Twin City trade name of Minneapolis Steel, and continued the Minneapolis name with threshers and other machinery. By 1940, however, the Minneapolis-Moline name was used exclusively.

Still not content to be outside the tractor market, Moline then purchased the Universal Tractor Company at Columbus, Ohio. This 1915 acquisition set the company back by $150,000. Initially, a two-cylinder machine was produced, but by 1918 the four-cylinder Moline Universal made its appearance, remaining on the market until 1923.

The Moline Universal was one of the most revolutionary tractors of its time and was one of the first row-crop tractors produced. In today's terminology, row-crop tractors generally have the connotation of a chassis with narrow front wheels and a pair of rear-drive wheels. Not so with the Moline Universal.

With this tractor, the drivers were ahead and the engine was nestled between them. A patented hitch arrangement permitted the operator to change from one implement to another with relative ease, and then permitted him to use the seat on the attached machine as his operating position. This concept permitted the relatively easy adaptation of horsedrawn implements to tractor power. A further advantage was that with the operator in the same location as when horses were used, the operating levers and controls and his vision of the job at hand were basically as before. Another couple of decades would pass before many implements would be developed specifically for farm tractor use.

So, the Moline Universal came and went in less than a decade. Its poor showing was due in part to the relatively poor acceptance of the design. Cost was also a factor. When a farmer could buy a Fordson for about one-third the money, why not buy a Fordson? As if these weren't problems enough, the postwar depression of the early 1920s created a financial squeeze, the likes of which hadn't been felt

in many a season. At this point, farmers would not or could not buy anything, regardless of price. With sales of all implements at record lows, and with inventories of high-capital items like tractors on hand, Moline Plow Co. came into desperate times by the early 1920s.

Financial elixir

John Willys had made promises of a financial elixir for this company of which he was the major stockholder. By 1921, however, Willys also found himself in financial straits with Willys-Overland. Without a transfusion from Willys, minor financial bleeding turned into a profuse hemorrhage. In 1919 the company had sold its interest in the Knight design to Root & Vandervoort Engineering Company at East Moline, Illinois. In turn, Moline Plow Co. bought out the R&V poppet-valve-engine line in 1921. Then in 1922 Moline Plow Company Incorporated appeared, being organized under the laws of the state of Virginia.

During 1922 and 1923 most of the assets were sold, and by 1925, only the Moline factory and the St. Louis Park plant remained on the ledgers. At this point the company was again reorganized as Moline Implement Company. With dogged persistence, the new company rose from corporate ashes to once again regain a position in the farm implement business.

Negotiations began in March 1929 between Moline Plow Co. and Minneapolis Steel & Machinery Co. Initially, these negotiations led to the formation of the Power Implement Company. When negotiations ended, Minneapolis Threshing Machine Co. was part of the organization. These three then comprised the Minneapolis-Moline Power Implement Company. Moline Plow ceased operations as such on May 16, 1929.

Minneapolis Steel & Machinery Company 1902–1929

Birth of the Twin City Tractor Line

Minneapolis Steel & Machinery (MS&M) was the youngest company of the three that formed Minneapolis-Moline. Despite the fact that it was not organized until 1902, MS&M nevertheless provided considerable color to the farm equipment industry.

Initially, MS&M was organized to fabricate steel sections for bridges, water towers and other structures. Shortly after being

The Twin City 40 from Minneapolis Steel & Machinery actually went into design during the early part of 1910. The earliest models used a 7 x 10 in. bore and stroke, rather than the 7¼ x 9 in. dimensions adopted in late 1911. Not until 1913 did the TC–40 assume its final form. A strong competitor with the Rumely OilPull and the Aultman-Taylor tractors, the TC–40 was tested at Nebraska in 1920 under Test Number 48. Production of this model ended in 1924.

organized the company began producing a line of stationary steam engines of the Corliss design. At this time virtually every manufacturing concern had its own powerplant and the majority of factory machinery was driven through a maze of lineshafts, belts and pulleys, helping to make sales of the Corliss engine quite satisfactory. This field was highly competitive by 1903, however, especially with Corliss engine specialists like Allis-Chalmers, Nordberg, Vilter, Frick and many others.

During 1904 MS&M ventured further into the heavy power business and sent some company representatives to Europe for an assessment of gas engine designs. Late that year the company purchased a Muenzel engine from G. Luther Company in Germany and subsequently erected it in the MS&M shops. From this engine, company engineers developed their own version of the Muenzel design.

It was tested in 1905 and was ready for the market in 1906. In the next five years, every effort was

During 1913 the Minneapolis Steel & Machinery Co. announced its 60–110 tractor. Within the next year it was downgraded to a 60–90, meaning that it developed 60 drawbar hp and 90 belt hp. This gigantic six-cylinder tractor weighed about 14 tons, and its 7¼ x 9 in. cylinders gave it a displacement of over 2200 ci. The TC–60 was listed as late as 1920, but production was not substantial. The 60–90 was used primarily for road building, plowing and similar duties. Of course, it had the belt horsepower to handle the largest thresher with ease. A single forward speed of 2 mph was provided, along with a reverse. With an engine of this size, the 100 gallon fuel tank was not oversized. The large canopy was designed more for the protection of the engine than for the comfort of the operator.

made to promote the Muenzel engine, but this department never made the money that was realized from the steel fabricating.

Twin City and Bull tractors

The move into tractor building came in 1910. Early that year it was decided to hire the Joy-Wilson Company of Minneapolis to design a new tractor, ordering five of them in February of that year. The new machine was to have a four-cylinder engine with a 7 x 10 in. bore and stroke. McVicker Engineering Company finished the drawings and the five tractors were to be completed by March 1911. In later years, McVicker claimed the credit for the design of the original Twin City tractor; this claim was also made by Jack Junkin, an engineer with MS&M at that time. Other historical records, however, place the credit for this design with Richard Rumlien, another MS&M engineer.

To the credit of this design it must be noted that the short-lived Advance tractor was undoubtedly designed by Junkin. This machine had a similar appearance to the Twin City. In addition, Reeves & Company at Columbus, Indiana, ordered a quantity of Twin City engines for use in their newly designed tractor. The Advance tractor barely got past the prototype stage when this firm was bought out by Rumely.

Additional work for the mechanical department came from a 1912 contract with J. I. Case Threshing Machine Company. This contract called for MS&M to build 500 of Case's 30-60 tractors. Presumably, MS&M had the manufacturing machinery and shop space for this project whereas Case probably did not.

Further bolstering the work in the MS&M shops was the manufacturing of the Bull tractor. In December 1913, Bull Company

contracted with MS&M to build 4,600 tractors at a price of $195 each, with Bull supplying the engines. This order for $887,000 in new work brightened the skies for MS&M. Now in addition to building their Twin City tractors, manufacturing capacity was run to its limit with production of the Bull tractors.

Bull wanted to buy the Hackney Manufacturing Company, a local firm that had been in the tractor business for several years but had never reaped great rewards for its efforts. MS&M did not purchase the Hackney plant, but J. L. Record, the president of MS&M, purchased a major interest in Hackney. This purchase later gave birth to the Toro Manufacturing Company, the firm which then built the engines for the Bull tractors. Toro is the Spanish word for bull, so with this the connection between Bull and Toro becomes obvious.

The contract with Bull was a most fortunate one for MS&M, especially since its sales of the big Twin City tractors were not all that they should have been. Part of the problem was in the relatively high price for these tractors. In 1915 the TC 60 sold for $4,200; the TC 40 was priced at $3,250; the TC 25 at $2,450; and the small TC 15 sold for

Bearing Chassis Number 5975, this rare 16–30 Twin City of 1918 is a remaining example of only 702 tractors built. This tractor demonstrated an attractive design compared to many of its contemporaries, but was plagued with starting problems and other difficulties. The enclosed body and the low lines of the 16–30 would soon be evident among other tractor builders, although this form was not generally used for another ten years. Owner Charles Doty of Princeton, Illinois, is sitting on the tractor.

$1,200. Even at these high prices the profits were rather small, considering the time and materials required for building the machines. Also to be considered were the tremendous design costs, an immense investment in foundry patterns, forging dies, jigs and other necessities. The problem boiled down to selling too much iron for too little money, and once the prairies were broken, the need for these huge tractors declined. Records indicate that in Iowa, for example, most of the big Twin City tractors were sold to county road departments rather than to farmers or threshermen.

In 1915 MS&M received a government contract to manufacture shell casings for the World War I effort. Until 1919, production of the Twin City tractors slowed considerably in favor of the government contract. In retrospect, this contract alone provided substantial income to MS&M at a time when many other farm equipment companies were investing their capital in new factories. With the postwar depression of the early 1920s, MS&M was ready to again enter the tractor business with a relatively sound position, while many of the established tractor builders found themselves with a mountain of bills and nothing with which to pay them.

Improving the Twin City tractor line

The Twin City Company was organized in 1915 as a sales arm for MS&M. This was their first organized effort to broaden the sales base. Through Twin City Co. came a series of branch houses and supply points, and this greatly enhanced the position of the Twin City line in the agricultural equipment industry.

Already in 1917 the company had decided on a conservative approach to the tractor business. No new models were in the wings, but under the guidance of Jack Junkin the existing models were somewhat improved. This included the use of a balanced and hardened crankshaft beginning with the 1918 models. In a curious footnote, Junkin was working on the design for the B. F. Avery tractor at the time of his death in 1936. A few years later, Minneapolis-Moline would acquire B. F. Avery and their small row-crop tractor.

After the cancellation of the war contracts in 1918, Twin City resumed the tractor business with cautious optimism. This resulted in the Twin City 12–20 model, introduced in 1919. The compact unit-frame design was indicative of the coming trend in farm tractors.

With the 12–20 came another revolutionary design. The four-cylinder engine had two intake and two exhaust valves per cylinder, permitting far greater capacity for intake and exhaust movement than could be achieved with a single-valve design. Details of this tractor's performance can be found in Nebraska Test Number 19.

In 1919 the company announced its entry into the motor truck business, and Jack Junkin finished the design of an entirely new all-steel thresher. Capping these events was the announcement of a new 20–35 tractor in September of 1919. When the book closed on the New Year's Eve of 1919 the company had already sold nearly 2,900 of the 12–20 tractors.

Forecasts for the merger

During 1920 MS&M found itself in tight financial straits, with this condition persisting into 1923. The following year saw a slight improvement and it now appeared that Twin City would weather the storm.

A new engine design for the 12–20 gave it a rating of 17 drawbar horsepower and 28 belt horsepower in 1924. The heavyweight designs were now dropped from the line and a new 27–44 model came in as a replacement for large power needs. Finally in 1929 came the Twin City 21–32 model.

During the 1929 transitional period from Minneapolis Steel to Minneapolis-Moline, the Model KT Twin City was also introduced. The MS&M contribution to the Minneapolis-Moline merger consisted of four tractor models: the KT, 17–28, 21–32 and 27–44. The Twin City all-steel thresher also became a part of the initial Minneapolis-Moline line. At the time of the merger, several sizes were available: the 22 x 36 Junior, 24 x 46, 28 x 46 Standard, 32 x 54 twelve-bar, 21 x 36, 28 x 48 and 28 x 46 Regular. A 28 x 46 Special was offered by Minneapolis-Moline in the 1934–36 period. The 36 x 64 sixteen-bar and the 40 x 64 sixteen-bar machines were offered only in 1932.

Minneapolis Steel & Machinery Co. faced identical problems to the other firms of the Minneapolis-Moline merger. The fast-changing agricultural implement industry was forcing them to expand tremendously and broaden the product line—or alternatively, to

Weighing 7,800 lb., the Twin City 16–30 tractor was equipped with the company's own four-cylinder engine, designed with a 5 x 7½ in. bore and stroke. Features included a Kingston carburetor and K-W high-tension magneto. On special order, this tractor could be equipped with electric starter and lights. Hyatt roller bearings were used throughout; this was a tremendous improvement over the plain bronze and Babbitt bearings of the past.

TWIN CITY 17-28 TRACTOR

A RECORD

"17-28—the tractor that proved that tractor life could be measured in decades rather than years—selling about as good as it did in 1919;" so said Farm Implement News in 1933.

3 Extra Years IS THE REPUTATION OF ALL **TWIN CITY** TRACTORS

The TWIN CITY "17-28" is truly the pioneer of modern tractor design and construction.

Of course, it has every worthwhile modern improvement. Owners claim the lowest cost per horse power for more years—and thousands have been in use for as many as 13, 14 and 15 years. The "17-28" has a reputation for *keeping* lubrication, fuel and upkeep *costs down low* all during its L-O-N-G LIFE. It has that FAMOUS 4-cylinder low speed Twin City engine with double air-cleaning, force feed lubrication, balanced crankshaft with 3 main bearings, double air-cleaning, water pump, large turbo-tube radiator cooling system with thermostatic temperature control. BURNS kerosene, gasoline or engine distillates without water injection. Besides, the "17-28" has all the other well-known Twin City features.

M-M Steel Wheels or Rubber Tired Wheels and other equipment to suit your needs.

Twin City "17-28" may also be bought especially equipped as a LISTER SPECIAL TRACTOR. Ask us for the facts and the bargain prices on this triple powered tractor—(Belt, drawbar, power takeoff).

TWIN CITY 27-44 TRACTOR

Except for size, power and a few details the TWIN CITY "27-44" is the same design as the Twin City "17-28."

It is one of the very few absolutely modern and up-to-date LARGE SIZE HEAVY DUTY TRACTORS.

If it's a lot of power, with a surplus of power over rating you need, see this Twin City. Easily pulls 5 or 6 14-inch bottoms—plowing deep, and has *surplus power* for the big belt jobs. Remember that the Twin City "27-44" has the *modern features* of the smaller size Twin City tractors. Gears are of nickel chromium steel —machine cut and heat treated—run in a bath of oil in a fully enclosed transmission case. See this powerful, low speed, long life Twin City Engine with force feed lubrication, automatic temperature control, 3-fuel carburetion (kerosene, gasoline, engine distillates without water injection), and a reputation for low cost operation that you'll like.

Previous page
Introduced for the 1929 market, the Twin City 21–32 was one of the last models developed by Minneapolis Steel & Machinery Co. The 1929 merger of this firm, along with Minneapolis Threshing Machine Co. and the Moline

Plow Co., yielded the new title of Minneapolis-Moline Power Implement Co. Also known as the Model FT, this tractor featured a four-cylinder engine with a rated speed of 1075 rpm, and used a 4½ x 6 in. bore and stroke. Production ran through 1934.

merge with another firm producing those products they needed. To be sure, the problems many of these companies faced were in part of their own making. But one problem was too big for any of them to solve alone: agriculture was becoming mechanized. With mechanization came an entirely new approach to agriculture with a new set of demands and requirements. Farmers were for the most part entirely willing to dispense with the labor-intensive methods of the past. During the transitional years of the 1920s and 1930s, farm equipment manufacturers were hard pressed to stay abreast of new developments, much less assume a leadership role. For this and other reasons, the assets of Minneapolis Steel & Machinery Co. were transferred to Minneapolis-Moline Power Implement Company on May 28, 1929.

A 1934 Minneapolis-Moline catalog illustrates the Twin City 17–28 tractor, left, noting that it had been on the market since 1919 and was still selling as well as it did at that time. At the time of this advertisement (1934) it could be furnished on steel wheels or rubber tires. It was also available as a Special Lister tractor, but no illustrations of this model have been located. This beautifully restored 21–32 tractor, right, is owned by Leo Andea of Dryden, Michigan. In 1989 it won the Best of the Show Award at the Mid-Iowa Antique Power Association Show at Marshalltown, Iowa, where these photos were taken. Beginning with the 1935 models, the 21–32 took the Model FTA title. The major change was an increased bore of 4⅝ inches; most other dimensions remained the same. Details of tractor performance can be found in Nebraska Test Numbers 152 and 270.

Listed from 1929 through 1935, the 27–44 was also known as the Model AT tractor, above. Its last published list price was $1,400. Features included a 5½ x 6¾ in., four-cylinder engine with a rated speed of 900 rpm. Removable sleeves were also featured. Designed for heavy belt and drawbar work, this tractor was capable of handling four plows or the largest thresher. It weighed 9,200 lb. Peeking under the hood of the 27–44 reveals the carburetor and manifold system,

right. Records from the Nebraska Tractor Test Laboratory reveal that this same basic tractor was tested in 1920 as the 20–35 model; it used a Holley 257 carburetor. When the 27–44 tractor was submitted for testing in 1926 under Test Number 122, a Schebler Model A carburetor was featured. This 27–44 is owned by Alex Gall of Oregon, Illinois, and has been displayed at the Northern Illinois Steam Power Club show.

MINNEAPOLIS 17-30 TYPE B TRACTOR
SPECIFICATIONS

Speed—Low, 2.33 M. P. H.—High, 3.05 M. P. H. —Reverse, 2.21 M. P. H.

Engine—4⅞" Bore—7" Stroke—4 Cylinder—Overhead Valve Type—Removable Cylinder Walls.

Pistons—Light Wt.—Grey Iron Casting—4 Rings.

Engine Speed—825 R. P. M.

Belt Pulley—15½" diameter — 7½" face — 825 R. P. M. Located on right hand side.

Crank Shaft—High Carbon Steel Forging—Heat treated—Ground—2¾" diameter—3 Bearings, Total Length 12".

Connecting Rods—Drop Forged—4 Bolt Type.

Camshaft—Hardened and Ground—3 Bearings, 2 7/16" Diam., Total Length 7½".

Lubrication System—Engine, Lubricator Pressure and Splash—Transmission, Oil Bath—Chassis, Alemite-Zerk.

Ignition System—Bosch High Tension with Impulse Starter.

Cooling System—Tubular Radiator Fan Cooled—Positive Water Circulation by Centrifugal Pump —Capacity 8½ gallons—Circulating Capacity 31¾ gallons per minute.

Governor—Enclosed Fly Ball Type.

Carburetion System—Efficient Carburetor for Kerosene or Gasoline—Heated and Hot Spot Manifold, Temperature Controlled—Water injection for heavy loads.

Clutch—Multiple Disc in Belt Pulley—Very accessible and easily adjusted.

Air Cleaner—Oil filter Type.

Transmission—Enclosed and Selective—Full Spur Gear Type—Gears are high Carbon Steel, Drop Forged, Machine Cut, Heat Treated.

Drive Wheels—53" diameter—12" face—Spade Lugs standard equipment.

Front Wheels—36" diameter—5" face mounted on Timken Bearings.

Power Take-Off—Speed, 527 R. P. M.—Extra Equipment see page 14.

Fuel—Gasoline tank capacity 6 gallons—Kerosene tank capacity 18 gallons.

General Dimensions—Overall Length—11'11".— Overall Width—6'4½"—Overall Height, 6'— Wheel Base, 7'6¾"—Center to Center of drive wheels, 58½"—Turning Radius, outside circle, 16'0".

Total Weight—Approximately 6800 pounds.

See following pages for description of parts and additional information. For Portable Engine see page 29.

Minneapolis Threshing Machine Company 1874–1929

Thoroughbred Line of Threshing Machines

Of the three companies that formed Minneapolis-Moline in 1929, Minneapolis Threshing Machine Co. (MTM) was the only one to have begun its career as a builder of grain threshers. For MTM, the roots go back to 1874 and a small factory at Fond du Lac, Wisconsin. Organized as Fond du Lac Threshing Machine Company, the new company soon got into financial difficulties. John S. McDonald, a major backer of the firm, then took over and renamed it McDonald Manufacturing Company. Its first offering, the

Minneapolis Threshing Machine Co. had entered the tractor business in 1911 and followed a conservative path in tractor design. To be sure, the Minneapolis tractors were of the highest quality, but the company seems to have done little toward the introduction of lightweight row-crop models during the 1920s. Typical of the period was this 17–30 cross-motor model.

Pride of the West apron-type threshing machine, was well received. It was replaced in the mid 1880s with the Victory vibrator-type machine. The company also built bobsleds, stump pullers and other items.

During 1887 the Minneapolis Threshing Machine Co. was organized. Capitalized at $250,000 the new firm secured the patents, patterns and equipment of McDonald Manufacturing Co. John McDonald contributed $60,000 in assets in exchange for stock in MTM. At this point, MTM did not build steam engines, but initially contracted with Huber Manufacturing Company of Marion, Ohio, to sell its engine. Through the 1890 season, MTM purchased both the Huber engines and the North Star engines from Upton Manufacturing Company at Port Huron, Michigan. During the first couple of years, boilers for Minneapolis engines were built mainly by the E. P. Allis Company

at West Allis, Wisconsin. Eventually, however, Minneapolis engines and boilers were built entirely on location at Hopkins, Minnesota, the site of the MTM factory.

Financial panic, expansion fever
Like the majority of American manufacturers, MTM suffered immensely from the great financial panic of 1893. After surviving these problems, the company continued improvements on its engines and threshers. The Columbian Victory thresher made its appearance in 1894, and Minneapolis engines were equipped with the Woolf valve gear. Tandem compound engines were also available.

In 1897, McDonald suggested that the company begin manufacturing gasoline engines under license from Otto Gasoline Engine Company at Philadelphia. The matter was studied at length, and it appears that MTM might have built and/or sold some Otto

"The Great Minneap

BUILT BY
THE MINNEAPOLIS THRESHING MACHINE COMPANY
WEST MINNEAPOLIS, HOPKINS, P. O., MINN.

THE

Line"

Cylinder Side

...POLIS SIMPLE TRACTION ENGINE ON DIRECT FLUE BOILER
...OOD, COAL AND STRAW BURNER, FLAT SPOKE
WHEELS, HEAVY PLOWING GEAR

engines, even going so far as to offer the Otto on a traction-gear chassis. This plan, if it did indeed materialize, never gained much headway. In 1900 the company advertised the Waterous gasoline engine, then being built by a St. Paul firm of that name. This too met with no success. For various reasons, McDonald was forced from the presidency of the company in 1897. Following him came F. E. Kenaston, and under his wise and conservative leadership the company remained strong for many years.

Expansion fever hit MTM in 1902. At this point the company bought a half-interest in the John Abell Engine & Machine Works Limited at Toronto, Ontario; the other half-interest was purchased by Advance Thresher Company at Battle Creek, Michigan. The whole idea was to provide a sound base for expansion into the Canadian market. When M. Rumely Company of LaPorte, Indiana, bought out Advance in 1911, MTM sold its interest in Abell to Rumely. For MTM, this was a tremendous opportunity, since it enabled the firm to unburden itself from an unwise purchase. The Abell plant taxed the company's financial reserves to the limit and required continuing investment in material and equipment. The bottom line was that the Abell plant was making a lot of red ink in the MTM

Of the three companies forming Minneapolis-Moline in 1929, only one had been among the old-line engine and thresher companies. Minneapolis Threshing Machine Co. had roots going back to 1874, and in 1891 added steam traction engines to its line. A 1910 catalog illustration typifies "The Great Minneapolis Line" of traction engines.

"The Great Minneapolis Line"

Belt Side

BUILT BY
THE MINNEAPOLIS THRESHING MACHINE COMPANY
WEST MINNEAPOLIS, HOPKINS, P. O., MINN.

THE MINNEAPOLIS SEPARATOR, FEEDER, NEW MINNEAPOLIS
GEARLESS WIND STACKER AND WEIGHER
FOLDED

The Great Minneapolis Line for 1910 included an extensive line of threshers that featured one of the largest separators ever built, a 44 x 72 in. model. These figures translate into a cylinder width of 44 in. and a separating width of 72 in., nearly twice as wide as was used on the ordinary midwestern farm. These huge threshers were intended for and used in wheat country and were powered by the largest steam engines.

ledgers. After getting out of this financial morass, Minneapolis Threshing Machine had expansion fever out of its system and waltzed to its own music until finally merging into Minneapolis-Moline in 1929.

Building only threshers—and building them well

Some historians believe that the old-line thresher builders held other implement manufacturers in disdain. On this basis, it is said that this accounts for the reason why few of them, MTM included, made no effort to become a full-line manufacturer. I believe an entirely different rationale must be used.

Virtually every thresher company started out in a crude shed or under a large shade tree. Simply put, that was the way of life. Most of these early manufacturers were skilled blacksmiths or

foundrymen, and some were skilled carpenters. Everything that was done was done by hand; the American craftsmen of the pre-Civil War period were doing things just like they had been done for centuries. Not until the 1860s did power tools assume any importance, and the advantage of power equipment did not make its appearance at the local blacksmith shop until the early 1900s.

Early thresher manufacturers concentrated their efforts, then, on making a single product and making it well. Reaper builders did the same, and many of the simple farm implements continued to be made on a local basis. Not until the 1890s did the concept of an expanded machinery line assume major importance among the manufacturers. Even then the usual practice was, for example, that a thresher company would contract with a plow company to

36

sell its plows. Perhaps a plow company would contract with a gas engine builder to sell its engines. This practice continued to some extent as late as the 1930s. In fact, the concept of a full-line company never reached fruition until the 1920s. With achievement of this goal by the largest firms, smaller short-line companies like MTM were forced either to look for a massive amount of capital to achieve full-line status, or as an alternative, to look toward a merger. The latter course is the one chosen by Minneapolis Threshing Machine Co.

In addition to its established steam engine and thresher business, MTM introduced a power corn sheller in 1902. This machine was very popular, and Minneapolis corn shellers remained in the line until the 1929 merger. Minneapolis-Moline then continued building corn shellers for many years.

Expansion into the tractor business

Recognizing the advance of the gasoline tractor as the coming scene in farm power, MTM began selling the Universal tractor in 1910. The following year, the company hired the services of Walter J. McVicker to design a new tractor. The McVicker design resulted in the 25-50 model of 1911 and 1912. Also announced was the 40-80 model, and then in 1914 came the smaller 20-40 size. The 40-80 remained in production for several years and was tested at Nebraska in 1920 under Test Number 15. As a result of these tests the 40-80 was downgraded to a 35-70 model. This size was apparently available on order until the 1929 merger.

In late 1915 MTM announced its new Model 15 tractor. This was its first small tractor and was undoubtedly designed in response to the tremendous demand for small tractors, as compared to giant behemoths like the 40-80. The 15 was also known as the 15-30 and was tested at Nebraska in May 1920. After these tests it too was downgraded to a 12-25 model and finally discontinued in 1926.

The 1920s saw the introduction of the 17-30 Type A and Type B tractors. Except for a slightly longer wheelbase on the Type B, these two models were nearly the same. Both models went into the 1929 merger. During the late 1920s MTM introduced two improved tractor models, the 27-42 and the 39-57. The 27-42 was tested at Nebraska under Test Number 162. This big 8,300 lb. tractor featured the company's own four-cylinder engine with a 4⅞ x 7 in. bore and stroke. The long-stroke design was a feature that Minneapolis-Moline later adhered to through its entire career in the tractor business.

Weighing nearly five tons, the 39-57 remained in the new Minneapolis-Moline line until existing stocks were sold. The huge four-cylinder Stearns engine had a 5½ x 6½ in. bore and stroke. Rated at 1000 rpm, it developed a maximum of 64½ belt horsepower, making the 39-57 one of the largest tractors on the 1929 market.

Minneapolis Threshing Machine Co. had developed a combine during the 1920s and this machine had an excellent reputation. The Minneapolis threshing machines were well respected, and the corn sheller was beyond reproach. Thus, MTM had

several well-established lines to offer in the merger in addition to its manufacturing capacity. The Minneapolis tractor line was phased out, however, in favor of the Twin City designs from Minneapolis Steel.

Prelude to the merger

During the turbulent 1920s, the postwar depression, the development of the radically different Farm-All row-crop tractor and the advent of implements designed specifically for tractor use created a nearly impossible situation for MTM. Without a major infusion of new capital, the company was unable to broaden its product line. The financial embarrassments of the early part of the decade continued to plague the firm. Being short of ready cash made it extremely difficult to expend the sums required for development of a competing row-crop tractor. Thus, Minneapolis Threshing Machine Co., like the other two parties of the Minneapolis-Moline triad, was not to have a row-crop design until the announcement of its M-M Universal MT tractor in 1931. It was tested that year at Nebraska under Test Number 197. This model became the parent of the M-M row-crop tractors.

It was almost by accident that Minneapolis Threshing became a part of Minneapolis-Moline. The original negotiations were between Moline Plow and Minneapolis Steel & Machinery. After learning of the possibility of a merger, MTM asked to become the third partner. Eventually this goal was achieved, and Minneapolis Threshing Machine became a part of Minneapolis-Moline.

Minneapolis-Moline Power Implement Company 1929–1949

A New Era of Mechanized Farming

The Minneapolis-Moline merger of 1929 brought together three companies that, if they had remained independent, probably would not have survived the Great Depression. As it was, the new company received the additional capital needed for new product lines and more efficient manufacturing methods. Obsolete or unneeded lines were phased out, and from virtually every aspect, Minneapolis-Moline presented itself

The Twin City MTA illustrated here is part of the Roger Mohr Collection at Vail, Iowa. These tractors were produced in the 1934–38 period, replacing the earlier MT model which had been introduced in 1931. Full details of this tractor's performance can be found in Nebraska Test Number 248. Brief specifications include a four-cylinder engine rated at 1150 rpm and using a 4¼ x 5 in. bore and stroke.

as an efficient, aggressive new company.

Initially, the line consisted of Minneapolis and Twin City tractor models, with the Minneapolis line being closed out after inventories were exhausted. The 17-28 closed out in 1935, as did the 27-44 model. KT, MT and FT tractors were built until 1934, and the following year they were replaced with the improved KTA, MTA and FTA models.

The Universal JT row-crop design appeared in 1934 and remained through 1937. Variations of this model included the JTS standard-tread (1936-37) and the JTO Orchard tractor built during the same period. The Universal Z made its appearance in 1936, and the Universal ZN had a 1938 debut, along with a standard-tread version of the Model Z tractor.

A wide selection of grain threshers remained in the line during the 1930s, but the major emphasis was on the combine. The

Model A 12 ft. combine had been available since 1929, being a carryover from the pre-merger days. Other sizes of the Model A included 16 and 20 ft. machines. The Model B was offered during 1929-30 in 10 and 12 ft. sizes, and the Model C was built during 1930. It could be purchased with 12, 16, or 20 ft. cutting heads. The Model D combines of 1930-31 were built in 10 and 12 ft. sizes.

Activities on the tillage implement scene were likewise in a state of flux. The rapidly changing requirements of tractor farming forced the abandonment of the majority of the tillage implements on the market. Although some patterns and forgings could be adapted to power farming implements, the vast majority were too light and too small to withstand the strains of tractor power.

In its own way, this transition from horsepower to tractor power was as revolutionary as the

A side view of the MTA tractor illustrates its relatively smooth lines for a tractor of 1935, on the previous pages. During the heyday of big tractors, manufacturers tended to build what they thought the farmers needed. During the lean Depression years of the 1930s, even the recalcitrants decided it was advisable to build what the farmers wanted. For this and other reasons, the 1930s saw revolutionary changes in power farming methods. One such innovation was this attractive Model MTA from the Roger Mohr Collection. On these pages, a Minneapolis-Moline Model KT tractor is shown here, silently rusting away somewhere in northern Wisconsin. Introduced in 1929, the Model KT was produced into 1934, at which time it was replaced with a slightly modified KTA tractor. The latter remained in production during 1938. During the transitional years following the Minneapolis-Moline merger, the first few tractors continued with the Twin City name cast into the radiator. After this supply was liquidated, the company put the Minneapolis-Twin City logo on the radiator and finally resolved the matter into the simple use of the famous M-M trademark.

computer revolution of recent times. Within recent memory the conversion of hand-operated mechanical typewriters and calculators to electronic brainpower is far in excess of anyone's wildest dreams. Just as we were plagued with pangs of conscience when junking the old Underwood typewriter and crank-operated calculator, the change was imperative if there was to be a chance at remaining competitive. From this perspective, then, farm implement manufacturers were driven by a great many forces over which they had no control. Despite a lack of control, however, the message was plain: change or quit! To the credit of Minneapolis-Moline and other implement builders of

the 1930s, they made the transition in remarkably good style, especially against the background of the Great Depression.

Just as farmers and farm equipment dealers alike were beginning to recover from the financial embarrassments of the 1930s, the rumblings of war came into earshot. After Pearl Harbor, virtually every manufacturing plant in the farm equipment industry was converted to war production, with only a few implements being built.

The inescapable conclusion is that World War II hastened the development of power farming methods immeasurably. Although power lifts were making their appearance prior to the war, the military demands of this conflict saw great strides in the development of hydraulic systems. After hostilities ended, manufacturers were in a position to apply this to countless nonmilitary applications. Along with the widespread use of hydraulics on tractors and farm machinery came yet another revolutionary advancement. Many steel alloys developed during the war found their way into farm machinery within a few years. This served to lighten the machine and reduced manufacturing costs.

Tractor style show and the Comfortractor

M-M made tractor history in September 1938. The company staged a "style" show in Minneapolis to introduce the most complete line of deluxe tractors ever seen before and more than 12,000 people attended. These included the Comfortractor and the Sport Open Model Roadster. Both models were equipped as much as possible like an automobile of the period. The Comfortractor was the first totally enclosed cab-type tractor ever put into regular production.

Later that year, Comfortractors were on display throughout the United States. Each M-M blockman traveled his territory in a Comfortractor, and in this way it came to every dealership in the country. Despite its advantages, the Comfortractor was about thirty years ahead of its time. Few farmers of the 1930s deemed it wise to work in the field in total comfort when their neighbors were toughing it out with open-air tractors. True enough, the Comfortractor was expensive, but beyond the factor of price, peer pressure undoubtedly kept some farmers from buying the tractor. A piece of family history partially confirms this theory. My father in law had fatal engine problems with his old Massey-Harris Challenger during World War II. The only tractor available to him at the time was a UDLX Comfortractor that had been on the dealer's lot for several months. Forced by necessity, he bought the UDLX and used it only until he was able to buy a conventional tractor after the war. So far as he was concerned, only sissies needed anything like the UDLX. This particular tractor was traded in and remained on the dealer's lot for several years and was finally scrapped.

When Minneapolis-Moline celebrated what it considered its 75th Anniversary in 1940, the tractor line was broad and well-equipped. The Standard line included the two-plow, optional enclosed cab RT; the two- to three-plow ZT; the three-plow UT; and the four- to five-plow GT. The all-purpose Universal tractor line included the two-row RTU; the two- to three-row ZTU; and the four-row UTU. Industrial tractors included the ZT1, UT1 and the GT1.

Innovative tractor design firsts

The Model R and Model Z tractors were equipped with a unique engine design that eliminated approximately 154 parts needed in conventional engines. By the use of a unique valve arrangement and combustion chamber design, the valves operated in a horizontal plane above the pistons. Long rocker arms contacted the camshaft at the lower end and the valve ends at the upper end, thus eliminating pushrods, lifters and other parts. By removing a large cover plate on the right-hand side of the engine, the operator was afforded easy adjustment of valve clearance. Removal of the small combustion chamber head on the left-hand side permitted the farmer to grind the valves with the grinding tool working in a horizontal position.

An added advantage to this cylinder head design was higher turbulence in the chambers for better combustion. This resulted in greater fuel efficiency and an increased horsepower output.

Minneapolis-Moline introduced the Z in the early summer of 1937. With this tractor came a new era in tractor design, particularly for M-M. Great emphasis was placed on easy and simple servicing of the engine. The Visionlined design was intended to provide the farmer with the best possible vision, essential when working in-row crops.

Thus, the 1930s were an eventful period for Minneapolis-Moline tractor design. Among the industry firsts were the totally enclosed cab, the first five-speed transmission and the first high-compression engine. For 1940 the compression ratio was in the range of 5.25:1, but an optional 4.31:1 low-compression head was available.

Martin Ronning was chief engineer for Minneapolis Threshing Machine Co. Prior to the M-M

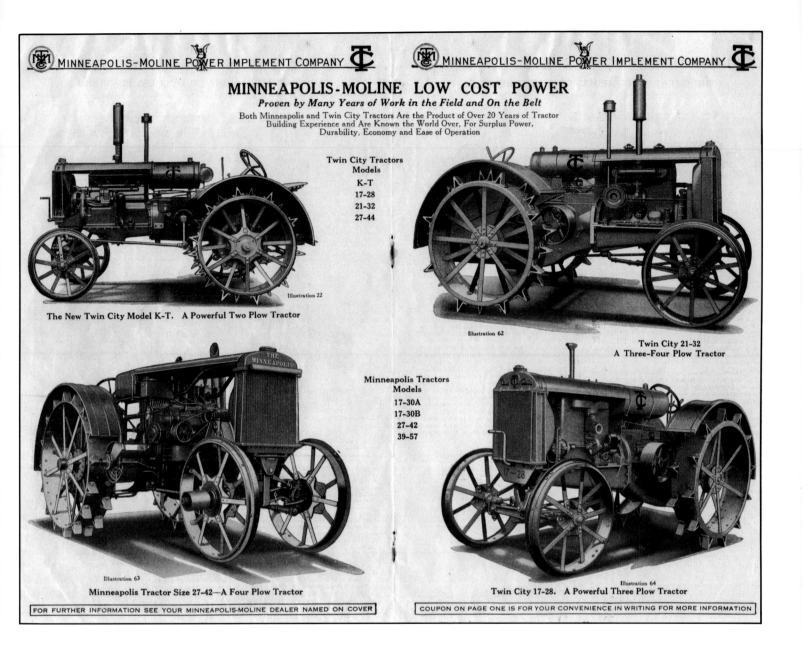

MINNEAPOLIS-MOLINE POWER IMPLEMENT COMPANY

MINNEAPOLIS-MOLINE POWER IMPLEMENT COMPANY

MINNEAPOLIS-MOLINE LOW COST POWER

Proven by Many Years of Work in the Field and On the Belt

Both Minneapolis and Twin City Tractors Are the Product of Over 20 Years of Tractor
Building Experience and Are Known the World Over, For Surplus Power,
Durability, Economy and Ease of Operation

Twin City Tractors
Models
K-T
17-28
21-32
27-44

Illustration 22

The New Twin City Model K-T. A Powerful Two Plow Tractor

Illustration 62

Twin City 21-32
A Three-Four Plow Tractor

Minneapolis Tractors
Models
17-30A
17-30B
27-42
39-57

Illustration 63

Minneapolis Tractor Size 27-42—A Four Plow Tractor

Illustration 64

Twin City 17-28. A Powerful Three Plow Tractor

FOR FURTHER INFORMATION SEE YOUR MINNEAPOLIS-MOLINE DEALER NAMED ON COVER

COUPON ON PAGE ONE IS FOR YOUR CONVENIENCE IN WRITING FOR MORE INFORMATION

merger, Ronning had plans ready for a new lightweight combine. After the merger, five years were spent in the laboratory, in the factory and on the farm testing the new design under every conceivable situation. Finally in late 1934 came the Model G Harvestor, with full production commencing in 1935. Ball and roller bearings were used extensively in the new machine. In addition, the design provided for wide interchangeability of parts within the machine itself. This kept parts inventory requirements to a minimum.

The extra capacity of the new Harvestor resulted partially from its higher sickle speed and an adjustable-speed reel drive. A rasp-bar cylinder was used, and the combination of a chain raddle and beaters ahead of the cylinder provided even feeding. An automatic self-leveling shoe was provided, and it kept the shoe in a level plane at all cutting elevations from 2 to 32 in. above the ground. During its first five years of

The 1930 Minneapolis-Moline catalog illustrates four of the tractors available for that season, including the Twin City K-T, 17–28 and 21–32 models. Also illustrated is the Minneapolis 27–42, a big tractor with a cross-mounted four-cylinder engine. In addition to this model, M-M also offered the Minneapolis 17–30A, 17–30B and 39–57 tractors. All of these models were being phased out, however, and sales were no doubt based on existing inventories.

THE GREAT MINNEAPOLIS LINE OF THRESHERS

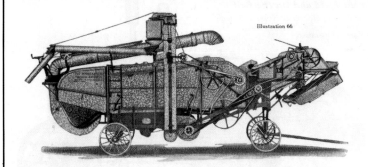

Illustration 66

Left Hand View of Minneapolis 24x46—28x46—32x54 Standard Steel Threshers

Minneapolis Threshers embrace all of the best principles that have been developed during over forty-two years of successful thresher manufacturing. They fully satisfy the demand for strong durable machines of the greatest efficiency in saving and cleaning grain. They excel on all the eight essentials of a good thresher.

1. **Adaptability**—Minneapolis Threshers will successfully thresh, save and clean all kinds of grains and seeds. They are so adjustable that only a few seeds require special attachments.

2. **Thorough Separation**—Efficient feeder, the large Keystone teeth, the large adjustable grate, the picker-beater, the lifting finger straw rack, the double chaffer and large sieve area give thorough separation and saves the grain.

3. **Ease of Operation**—Minneapolis Threshers do not require hair-splitting adjustments. Simple adjustments enable beginners to successfully thresh, clean and save grain.

4. **Capacity**—Greater length, better separating devices and larger space over straw rack and in cleaning shoe give greater capacity.

5. **Light Running**—Carefully balanced cylinder, Rockwood pulleys, 12 roller bearings, scientifically balanced straw rack, return pan, grain pan and shoe means less vibration, light running and less power required.

6. **Long Life**—Rigid steel frame, rust resisting materials, oversize parts and quality materials give years of service.

7. **Low Upkeep Cost**—Scientific design and precision workmanship built into Minneapolis threshers has lowered their upkeep cost to the minimum.

8. **Dependability**—Parts built oversize rather than small to lower the price of the machine, and highest quality materials assure that Minneapolis threshers are ready to run and will save the grain season after season.

Minneapolis Threshers are built in eight sizes: 22x36, 24x46, 28x46, 32x54 with 12 bar cylinders and 32x54, 36x58, 36x64, 40x64 with 16 bar cylinders.

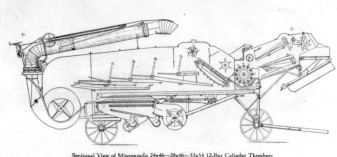

Sectional View of Minneapolis 24x46—28x46—32x54 12-Bar Cylinder Threshers

FOR FURTHER INFORMATION SEE YOUR MINNEAPOLIS-MOLINE DEALER NAMED ON COVER

MINNEAPOLIS-MOLINE POWER IMPLEMENT COMPANY | TC

Twin City All-Steel Threshers
Sizes 21x36, 28x46, 28x48

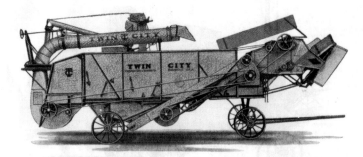

Illustration 68   Right Hand View of Twin City 28-46 Thresher

Twin City All Steel Threshers are built to do all threshing jobs on the farm from the smallest to largest seed with but few seeds requiring special attachments. They are known all over the grain growing sections for grain saving qualities; economical, dependable service and simple operation.

Long Life Features built into Twin City Threshers:

Frame—Heavy angles, rigidly braced, hot riveted, all bearings mounted on frame members—all sheet metal parts, special steel, heavy galvanized coated, for TWIN CITY threshers.

Bearings—Anti-friction roller bearings on important drives.

Cylinder—Heavy duty—double bar fitted with high carbon drop forged, heat treated teeth, accurately balanced, mounted on self-aligning Timken bearings.

Auxiliary Cylinder—Small cylinder mounted on main cylinder shaft, fitted with corrugated teeth re-threshes all tailings and delivers them on the grain pan—smaller in diameter prevents cracking grain. Exclusive Twin City feature.

Straw Racks—Big capacity, heavy gauge, thick galvanized coated steel, pressed louvre type which keeps short straw on straw rack prevents loading chaffer.

Grain Pan—heavy gauge, corrugated, positively moves grain and chaff evenly to grain cleaning shoe.

Cleaning Fan—Four blades deliver large even volume of air, so necessary for cleaning grain.

Grain Shoe—Large capacity, fitted with no-choke chaffer adjustable sieve; also brackets to take special sieves when needed.

Stacker—Blower, fan housing hinged for accessibility.

Twin City threshers built in 3 sizes: 21-36, 28-46, 28-48.

Sectional View of Twin City 28x46 All Steel Thresher

COUPON ON PAGE ONE IS FOR YOUR CONVENIENCE IN WRITING FOR MORE INFORMATION

Grain threshers came into the Minneapolis-Moline line from the old Twin City series. Jack Junkin had designed the Twin City thresher in about 1920, and these machines were chosen rather than those from Minneapolis Threshing Machine Co. These 1930 catalog illustrations show the Regular and Standard series threshing machines. Note the heading of this advertisement, with the trademarks of the three merged companies superimposed over the words Minneapolis-Moline Power Implement Company.

production the Harvestor was completely sold out, even though the factory operated at its maximum capacity.

Late in 1936 M-M announced the Harvestor Junior with either a 6 ft. or an 8 ft. cut. The larger model weighed but 3,950 lb., including the auxiliary engine.

In 1940 Minneapolis-Moline announced its new Model 69 Harvestor, offering 'straight-through' design. The model designation was derived from the fact that the divider points were

exactly 69 in. apart. A major feature of the Model 69 was the introduction of longer guard fingers and the use of stub-type sickle sections to eliminate clogging problems. The Model 69 was designed for use with the Model R tractor and others of similar horsepower.

During the 1930s M-M engineers developed the Huskor, a lightweight corn picker designed for one-person operation. An interesting feature of the early design is the use of a twelve-roll

MINNEAPOLIS-MOLINE POWER IMPLEMENT COMPANY

Minneapolis Combines

Illustration 69

Left Hand View of Minneapolis Model "A" Combine

Minneapolis-Moline Combines in four sizes give grain growers a selection to meet their requirements.

Model A—16-foot cutting bar which may be fitted with 4-foot light crop extension; threshing unit, 24x42.

Model B—10-foot cutting bar which may be fitted with 2-foot light crop extension; threshing unit, 22x36.

Model C-16—16-foot cutting bar; threshing unit, 28x46.

Model C-20—20-foot heavy cutting bar; threshing unit, 28x46.

Pickups may be supplied for all the above combines. Windrowers are supplied in 16-foot or 20-foot cuts.

Minneapolis Combines are designed to meet the severest conditions. A few of their long life and grain-saving features are:

Large Feeder House With Big Capacity—will not choke up.

Double Barred Cylinder With Steel Heads—fitted with Minneapolis special Keystone teeth—mounted on ball bearings.

Semi-Rotary Straw Racks—with action that thins the straw in travel—agitates the straw from cylinder to spreader.

Large Capacity Shoe and Recleaner—saves light as well as heavy grain and delivers clean grain into tank.

Frame—heavy channels and angle steel, rigidly braced—with all bearings mounted on frame.

Steel Chain Positive Drive—with safety clutches at important points.

Surplus Powered—by large oversized motors which deliver steady power for all conditions.

Alemite-Zerk Lubrication.

The Weight—well distributed over wheels which makes it a light draft machine.

Simple and Easy to Adjust and Operate.

Operator's Platform—located on deck out of the dust where operator can watch grain bin, cutting bar and both sides of machine.

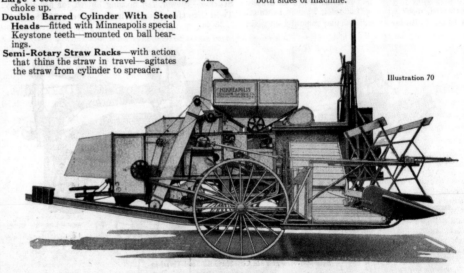

Illustration 70

Right Hand View of Minneapolis Model "B" Combine

FOR FURTHER INFORMATION SEE YOUR MINNEAPOLIS-MOLINE DEALER NAMED ON COVER

Several sizes of combines were initially offered by Minneapolis-Moline, right. These had already been marketed by Minneapolis Threshing Machine. This firm also had pioneered the development of the cylinder-type corn sheller and it, too, came into the M-M line. The illustrations are from a 1930 catalog. Built from 1934 to 1937, on the next pages, the Universal J tractor was thus named because it was "suited to all purposes and condition and adapted to a great variety of uses." Weighing but 3,450 lb., it featured a five-speed gearbox, oil-bath air cleaner and a large oil filter. The Universal J tractor featured a 196 ci, four-cylinder engine. Rated at 1275 rpm, it used a 3⅝ x 4¾ in. bore and stroke. Individual Bendix-style brakes were standard equipment, and when equipped with rubber tires, road speeds of up to 18 mph could be attained. When equipped with steel wheels, however, the high speed was locked out for the safety of the operator.

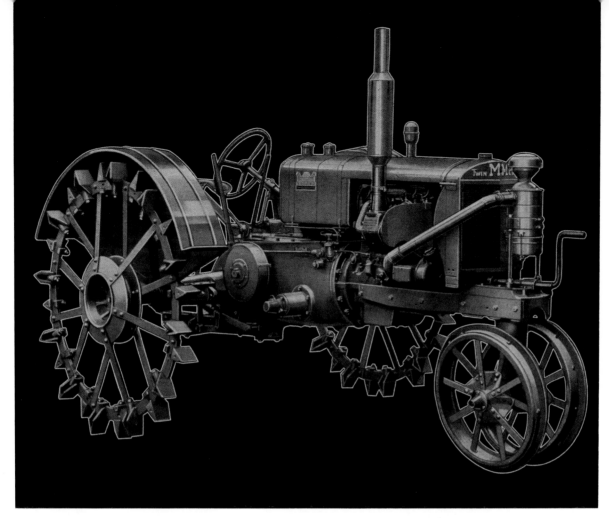

THE NEW UNIVERSAL "J" WITH

The name "UNIVERSAL" means "suited to all purposes and conditions and adapted to a great variety of uses." This new TWIN CITY Model "J" tractor is named UNIVERSAL because, on your farm, it will do all that the name says.

The "J" is a *neat, compact, simple,* and *powerful* 2-3 plow tractor.

It gives you 4 kinds of power! *Drawbar, Power Take-off, Belt,* and *Power Lift.* The "J" WEIGHS ONLY 3450 LBS. with steel wheels and lugs.

The powerful 4-cylinder HEAVY DUTY MOTOR is built to stand the gaff, and has every proved modern feature. You'll especially like the *patented* 3-FUEL MANIFOLD which efficiently handles gasoline, kerosene, and engine distillates without water injection.

This *new* TWIN CITY has 5 forward speeds—4 practical Field speeds and a high road speed. With these and variable speed governor controlled from the seat, you can travel from a crawl to 12.2 miles per hour to suit the job you're doing.

The travel speed can be increased by adjusting governor when the "J" is used for hauling and is equipped with rubber tires.

Every one of these speeds is a *practical speed* for some farm or hauling operation.

Shifting gears is as easy as in a modern automobile.

The UNIVERSAL "J" is carefully sealed against entrance of dust or oil leakage. Shafts coming out of the transmission are double sealed with the most modern seals to eliminate oil leaks.

Notice the filter type breather, the large size oil filter, the modern oil wash air cleaner, the gasoline filter, the enclosed magneto, the double sealed bearings, etc., etc.

The transmission is quiet with cut gears made of alloy steel and heat treated for long life.

Roller and ball bearings at all vital points assure long life.

Remember, TWIN CITY tractors have been built along the same basic lines of design for 3 years longer than any tractor still in production; and MOLINE was *first to build a complete line of UNIVERSAL machinery for quick direct attachment to a tractor.* These long years of experience mean a lot to any one buying a UNIVERSAL "J" and its modern power lift implements which are the easiest to put on or take off.

"CULTIVATES 2 OR 4 ROWS"

"BUILT TO DO ALL THE WORK"

ADVANTAGES

THE UNIVERSAL "J" gives you the ADVANTAGES of both Standard and Wide Tread Tractors.

PERFORMANCE

The "J" is a sensational, proved performer in the field, in row crops, on the belt, and on the road. It's a year around tractor.

"TOE-TIP" POWER-LIFT

"Quick-on—Quick-off"
UNIVERSAL MACHINES
Backed by Years of Success

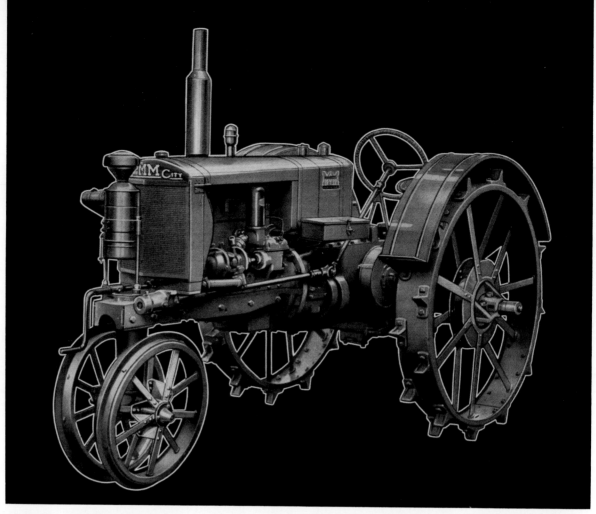

5 FORWARD SPEEDS and ADJUSTABLE TREAD

The rear wheels of the Universal "J" are clamped on the "Live" rear axle—and may easily be adjusted for tread on the axle. Even after being in one place for a long time a change is easy to make. The wheels are also reversible. NO EXTRA PARTS OR ATTACHMENTS ARE NEEDED TO CHANGE TREADS.

The wheels are easily adjusted to obtain a 54, 56¼, 58½, 60¾, 63, 67, 69¼, 71½, 73¾, or 76" wheel tread, (center to center measurements). Adjustments, being easy, are quickly made. *You can plow without side draft* and *cultivate narrow or wide spaced rows*—2 or 4 rows at a time. The fenders are adjusted in and out with the wheels to protect operator from dust.

Guard rims are available for the open type rear wheels to allow operating on highways. Reversible, cast "V" shaped front wheels are also available for use in trenches or on ridges.

"PLOWS WITHOUT SIDE DRAFT"

The "J" handles as easily as a modern automobile. The modern 3-spoke steering wheel has a sure grip *composition rim* that is easy on the hands in both hot and cold weather.

The steering gear is quick acting and steering is easy—just try it. The worm and sector gears mounted on roller bearings, are located in the front pedestal and run in oil. See Page 8 for details.

The "J" can be instantly stopped, even when going in high with a load, by means of 2 large brakes. The Universal "J" turns in a circle with less than a 7 ft. radius using one of the brakes. When equipped with rubber tires and tractor is used for high speed hauling, a single foot pedal to operate both brakes is available so that tractor and load can be stopped instantly without swerving since equal braking pressure is applied to each wheel. The "J" is built for safety as well as good work.

The "J" seat is of a new comfortable, safe design. A large rubber block cushions the side sway as well as the up and down movements.

Take a look at the *slip-proof,* roomy steel platform. All controls are easily reached whether sitting on seat, standing on platform, or standing on ground when backing up to implements and you can always see the work you're doing.

The fuel tank is narrow and sides of the tractor are free from obstructions. The seat is up just high enough for good vision, yet not too high for safe operation. The Universal "J" has movable fenders to protect operator from dust. There is nothing above the front wheels but the "sky" so clogging is hardly possible.

Here is a modern tractor built for safety, comfort, and easy operation as well as year around usefulness and economy.

"BUILT TO DO ALL THE WORK"

husking bed at a time when eight husking rolls were the industry standard. As with the Harvestor combines, the Huskor made extensive use of ball and roller bearings.

Minneapolis-Moline was busy during the 1930s with the design of a new tillage line. By 1940 the AF and DF series of tractor plows were on the market. Both featured a high lift and high clearance. The smaller AF was available in two- and three-bottom sizes, while the larger DF was built in three-, four- and five-bottom models.

Another innovative design was the TV plow, an integral two-way plow for the Model R tractor. It had obvious advantages in irrigation farming, hillside plowing, terracing and other situations where back furrows or dead furrows were inadvisable.

Having its roots with the Moline Universal of the 1920s, the Uni-Carrier of the 1930s was a two-wheel unit that was hitched to the tractor. Built somewhat like a plow frame, it was equipped with power lift and a friction release. On this frame was a tool bar to which could be attached a variety of Uni-Tiller implements.

Also receiving special attention in the 1930s were innovative corn planter designs, listers, lister-planters and grain drills. By 1940 the Moline-Monitor grain drills were of all-steel construction and featured high-carbon steel wherever necessary to reduce weight.

In about 1902 the Minneapolis Threshing Machine Co. had introduced a cylinder-type corn sheller. From the beginning, Minneapolis shellers gained a high reputation, coming into the M-M merger and seeing many improvements during the 1930s. By 1940 the M-M corn sheller line included the Model A, Model B and Model D machines, all of cylinder design but with varying capacities. For example, the Model A was rated at 800 bushels per hour, and the Model B was capable of up to 1,400 bushels per hour. The smaller Model D was intended for the average farm and had a capacity of 275 bushels per hour.

Minneapolis-Moline pioneered the use of LP-gas as a tractor fuel beginning in the early 1940s. Tractors were optionally available with factory-installed LP-gas equipment until M-M finally merged to form White Farm Equipment.

Minneapolis-Moline Visionlined tractors provided a new approach toward improved operator visibility. This was especially important with row-crop tractors. An overhead view illustrates the muffler squarely in the center of the hood, leaving each side unobstructed. Several front-axle options were available, including this single-wheel version. On the next pages, during the 1930s, Allis-Chalmers changed from a dark green color to Persian Orange, J. I. Case changed from bluish gray to Flambeau Red and Massey-Harris changed from steel gray to a bright red. These changes were ostensibly intended to make the tractors more visible, more attractive and ultimately, more salable. Minneapolis-Moline likewise followed suit by changing from a gray finish to its now-famous Prairie Gold. This attractively restored Model ZTS standard-tread tractor is part of the Roger Mohr Collection.

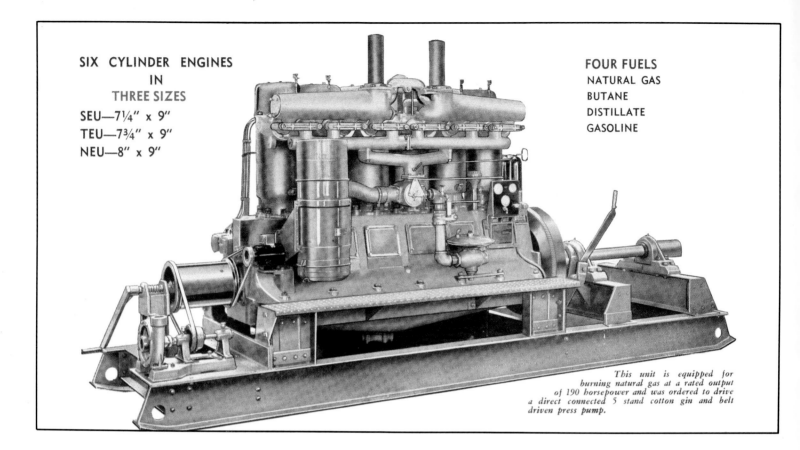

SIX CYLINDER ENGINES
IN
THREE SIZES
SEU—7¼" x 9"
TEU—7¾" x 9"
NEU—8" x 9"

FOUR FUELS
NATURAL GAS
BUTANE
DISTILLATE
GASOLINE

This unit is equipped for burning natural gas at a rated output of 190 horsepower and was ordered to drive a direct connected 5 stand cotton gin and belt driven press pump.

Although it is generally thought that the large engines as used in the Twin City 40 tractor ended with production of this unit, a 1940 advertisement, above, shows that derivations were still available at that time. All of six-cylinder design, these engines were built in three sizes and had ratings of 182, 208 and 221 hp at a speed of 650 rpm. Introduced in 1937, the RU and EU power units were but a small part of an extensive line, right. Minneapolis-Moline produced this advertisement in 1940. The Minneapolis-Moline Z series tractors were popular right from the beginning of production, on the next page. The row-crop style Model ZT was tested at Nebraska in 1937 under Test Number 290. In this test, distillate fuel was used. Test Number 352 of 1940 used a tractor that was virtually identical, except that gasoline was the chosen fuel. As might be expected, a substantially greater horsepower output was achieved. Minneapolis offered the Z series in several configurations, including several row-crop styles and this rather rare standard-tread model.

The New RU And EU Series MM Twin City Power Units
The Sensational New Utility Engine

2 Sizes
RU SERIES
3⅝" x 4½"
4 CYLINDER

EU SERIES
3⅝" x 4"
4 CYLINDER

4 Fuels
NATURAL GAS
BUTANE
DISTILLATE
GASOLINE

3 Models
IN EACH SIZE

MODEL "A"
WITH ENCLOSURES AND COOLING SYSTEM

MODEL "B"
WITHOUT ENCLOSURES WITH COOLING SYSTEM

MODEL "D"
WITHOUT ENCLOSURES OR COOLING SYSTEM

FUEL TANK FOR USE
WITH LIQUID FUELS CAN BE INCLUDED WITH OR OMITTED FROM ANY MODEL

Economical–Dependable

Although these unique engines were introduced in 1937, they were proved products to the famous MM Engineering Department, so thoroughly did they check and prove these engines under thousands of hours of gruelling work. Since that date, thousands of these engines have been purchased by discriminating buyers over the whole world, which in itself is evidence of the new standard which these engines have set for this class of power.

Sturdy–Long Life

These MM engines are delivered complete ready to burn your cheapest fuel. They are equipped with an automatic ground switch (see page 3), gauges, electric starting (optional), muffler, governor, in fact everything to make the unit ready for service. When power is needed, investigate these utility units. Note the portability, the compactness, the economy. Compare these engines with others in the same power class and see the difference. MM engines are built to do the work.

When it was introduced in 1938, the Model UDLX Comfortractor was one of the most widely publicized tractors of its time. Although the competing manufacturers had made great strides in customizing and streamlining their tractors, no one in the industry came close to duplicating this totally enclosed design. It had five forward speeds from a crawl up to 40 mph, ostensibly making this tractor a field workhorse by day and still suitable for an evening meeting in town.

A head-on view of the UDLX tractor illustrates its sleek lines, dual headlights and automotive-style grillework, above. These tractors used the same engine as the Model U series, and in fact, the high-compression engine developed by Minneapolis-Moline was instrumental in setting new standards for the industry. M-M claimed to have been the first to sell high-compression tractor engines to farmers, beginning in the spring of 1935. The rear view, on the next page, of the UDLX tractor illustrates the large doors for easy access to the operator compartment. Other features included an impact-resistant and insulated cab, safety glass, windshield wipers, radio, heater, defroster and foot accelerator. Despite the great attention it received in the farm press, the UDLX was not at all popular with farmers. This and its relatively high price tag of $2,155 held sales to only about 150 units between 1938 and 1941. It was nearly 30 years before the totally enclosed cab gained genuine popularity.

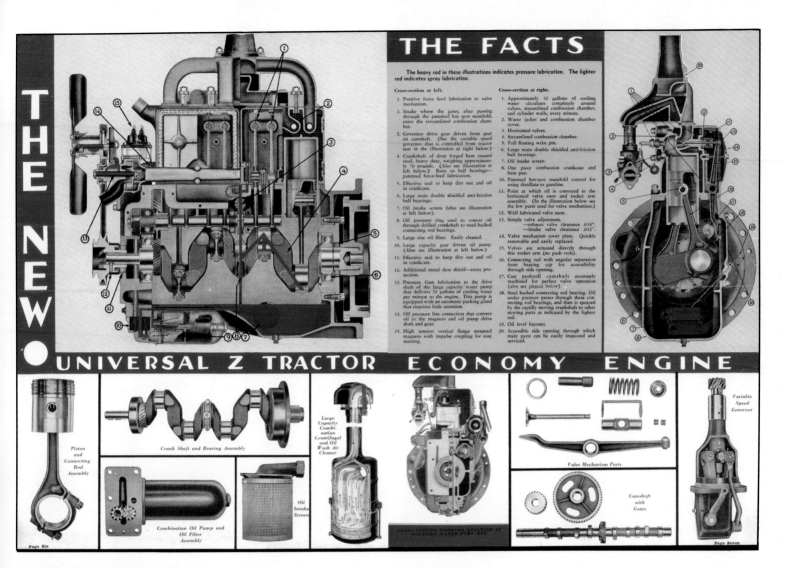

A look at the cab and dashboard of the UDLX shows an impressive instrument panel, left. Comparing the visibility from the cab with automotive design of the pre-war period, the UDLX didn't fare too badly on that score either. Of the few UDLX tractors built, only a handful remain, making the UDLX one of the most collectible of the Minneapolis-Moline tractor line. This particular example finds its home in the Roger Mohr Collection. A 1939 catalog illustrates a cross section of the Universal Z tractor engine, above. Note the unique horizontal valve arrangement and the extended rocker arms.

61

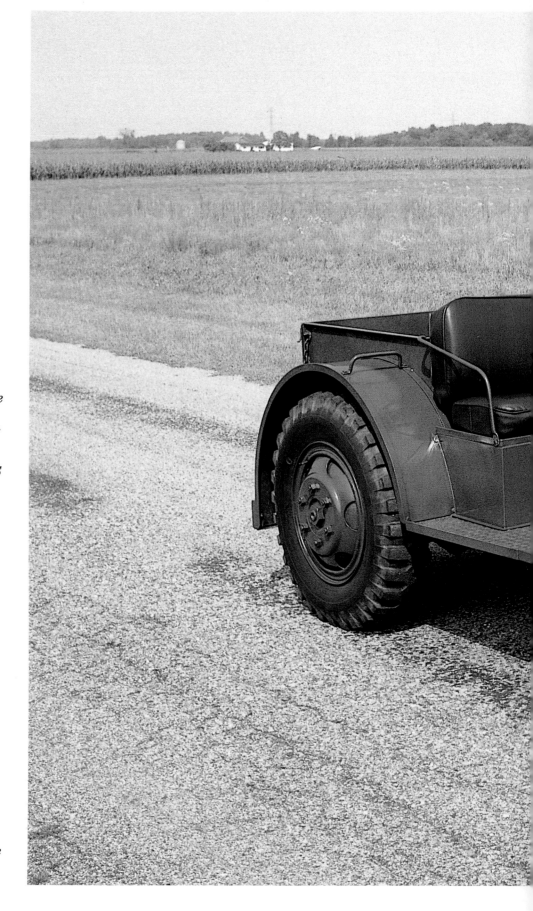

Rated at approximately 32 belt hp, the Z series tractors were an important and integral part of the M-M line for a number of years, on the previous pages. Production of the ZTU-ZTN models ran from 1940 to 1948; the ZTS was built from 1940 to 1947; the ZAU series ran from 1949 to 1952; and the ZAS models were produced in the 1949–53 period. In addition to the above styles were the ZAE, manufactured from 1949 to 1952; the ZAN, offered from 1949 to 1952; and the ZB model of 1953. The styling of this prewar Model Z illustrates the streamlined design of all M-M models of this period. Built by Minneapolis-Moline in 1944 under contract with the US Navy, on these pages, this M-M Jeep is owned by Ernest Weissert of Bourbon, Indiana. According to a 1944 M-M catalog, "The name JEEP was first given to an Army tractor by a Minnesota National Guardsman in the summer of 1940, and is not a contraction of the two words 'General Purpose' (GP) but was taken from the Popeye cartoons. The author of the cartoon created a character called the Jeep which knew all the answers and could do many unusual things." Minneapolis-Moline began work on the conversion of farm tractors into military vehicles as early as 1938.

A very rare tractor, the Model YT was produced in 1937. This prototype, one of three built, is owned by Dan Shima of Eldridge, Iowa. The YT used a two-cylinder engine, basically a Model R engine that was cut in half. Perhaps M-M envisioned this tractor as a possible competitor to the Farmall F–12 or the John Deere B, and reasoned that if it was successful, the company could produce this model with a minimum expenditure for retooling. Whatever the logic might have been, the experiment was a failure.

A close-up view of the Model YT tractor illustrates the two-cylinder engine, it simply being half of the Model R engine. This prototype shows the crude manner in which the engine was divided, and a close look shows a hand-built exhaust pipe. Minneapolis-Moline built only 25 of the Model YT tractors in 1937, and all were returned to the factory. Quite possibly this is the only remaining example of a tractor model that might have been.

This beautifully restored Model UTU tractor of 1939, on the previous pages, is a part of the Roger Mohr Collection. The UTU remained in production until 1953. Always looking for innovative ideas, M-M engineers produced the first factory-built LP-gas tractors in 1941. Citing such advantages as low fuel cost, excellent fuel economy and lower engine maintenance, this concept was soon put into practice by competing companies. Nebraska Test Number 319 provides detailed information on the fuel economy and drawbar performance of this model. Briefly, its specifications included a four-cylinder engine having a 4¼ x 5 in. bore and stroke. For 1948 this tractor retailed at $1,782 on rubber, but could also be purchased on steel wheels for $1,586. The Minneapolis-Moline Model

U Standard-Tread series (UTS) was first sold in 1940, above, apparently remaining in production until 1953. It used the same Minneapolis-built four-cylinder engine as found in other models of the U series tractors, namely, four cylinders with a bore of 4¼ in. and a stroke of 5 in. In 1948 it carried a list price of $1,787. The extra heavy cast-iron frame carrying the front axle is evident. The Model UTS tractor could be furnished with rubber tires or with steel wheels, at the wish of the customer, right. During World War II, the relatively few farm tractors produced were often on steel, simply because rubber was not available. Nebraska Test Numbers 310 and 311 of 1938 note 39 drawbar hp on gasoline fuel, and slightly over 32 hp using distillate. This fuel was heavily promoted during the 1930s

and 1940s as an alternative to gasoline with its higher cost, and kerosene with its obvious pre-ignition problems. Due to the loss of horsepower experienced with distillate, along with crankcase dilution and shortened engine life, most farmers opted for gasoline fuel by the 1950s. Soon this choice was again altered with the introduction of highly efficient diesels.

70

Not a farm tractor at all, this ZTX of 1943 was built for the US military in World War II. The engine and chassis were similar to that used in the ZTS farm tractor, but the cab was that of the Model RT. A five-speed gearbox offered a top speed of 15.3 mph. Only 25 of these tractors were built, and this one is in the Roger Mohr Collection.

The heavy grille is one of the unique features of this ZTX tractor. Minneapolis-Moline, like other farm equipment manufacturers, turned its attention to military production during World War II. In this particular case, components of the ZTS and RT tractors were used, along with other such modifications as necessary for military service.

This M-M RTU of 1949 vintage, on the previous pages, was photographed at the Mid-Iowa Antique Power Association Show in 1989. Owned by Jim Adams of Marshalltown, Iowa, this nicely restored tractor typifies the R-series tractors of the period. Introduced in 1939 as the RT model, the following year saw the introduction of the RTU, RTN, RTI and RTS models, all derivations of the same basic design, but intended for various specific applications. The Model RTU featured a four-cylinder engine with a 3⅝ x 4 in. bore and stroke, above. The horizontal valves were operated by long rocker arms, and the two-bearing crankshaft featured a roller bearing for the front main. The design was intended to permit engine maintenance without the necessity of its being completely dismantled. Originally rated at 1400 rpm, the RTU was tested at Nebraska in 1940 under Test Number 341. In 1951 the Model R was again tested (Test Number 468), but in this instance a rated speed of 1500 rpm was used. Typical of the instrumentation for the Minneapolis-Moline tractors of the 1940s is this RTU model, right. Since electric starting and lighting was featured, the ammeter was standard equipment, as was the water temperature gauge and the oil pressure gauge. A combination switch was used to start and stop the engine, along with control of the electric lights.

A pioneer of innovation, this M-M Model R of 1944 was equipped with a cab and included dual selective hydraulics for the cultivator. Very successful throughout its long production run of 1939 to 1955, the Model R series featured a 24 hp, four-cylinder engine. Priced at approximately $1,500, the Model R was available in several chassis and wheel arrangements to suit specific crops and farming practices.

A rear view of the M-M Model R of 1944 illustrates the cab arrangement. Although tractor cabs did not gain major importance for some years, this innovation is now widely used. The cleverly designed engine of this tractor model permitted virtually a complete overhaul without the necessity of splitting the tractor. This feature alone was a major step forward in tractor engineering.

Introduced in 1938, the U-series tractors remained in production until 1957. This style used a four-cylinder engine of overhead-valve design, featuring a 4¼ x 5 in. bore and stroke. In order to minimize previous problems with gasket leakage, and also to provide easier maintenance, this four-cylinder engine was designed with the cylinders cast in pairs. Thus, a cracked valve seat or other serious problem that otherwise would have required a new four-cylinder head needed but half that amount. From 1953 to 1957 this tractor could also be purchased with the M-M diesel engine. The gasoline model could be furnished for use with LP-gas at an additional $229 over the standard list price of $2,278.

With a maximum output of 56 belt hp, the big Model G tractor was designed for the heaviest farm work. Introduced in 1940, this model was slightly revamped as the GTA tractor shown here and was thus produced from 1942 to 1947. Following this series was the GTB with a production run of 1947–53. Also available between 1951 and 1953 was the GTC tractor, virtually identical to the GTB, except that it was factory-equipped for burning LP-gas. Only the GT models used a red grille; the GTA and its descendants used a yellow grille. This 1946 model GTA is a part of the Roger Mohr Collection.

This RTE tractor of 1949 vintage is also owned by Roger Mohr. Built from 1948 to 1953, these tractors featured the Minneapolis-Moline Model EE engine. Rated at 24 hp, it had a maximum operating speed of 1500 rpm. From all appearances, the RTE model did not meet with the tremendous sales success shared by some of the other models, thus explaining the relatively short production run. An overhead view of a 1949 Model RTE tractor illustrates its use with a Minneapolis-Moline Model LS spreader, on the next pages. With its 24 hp engine, the RTE was an ideal size for use with the spreader and other light farm duties. During the late 1940s, farm tractor builders became obsessed with the notion that every farm needed at least two of these handy little workers. Within a few years an entirely new trend was established toward larger tractors, rather than smaller models.

Originally built for the US Air Force, above, this M-M Model RTI-Military tractor now resides in the Roger Mohr Collection. M-M developed this military design of its RTI Industrial tractor for use during the Korean conflict. It is equipped with lifting lugs for crane loading. A close-up of the nameplate for the RTI-Military tractor, left, provides the necessary data required by the Armed Forces.

Weighing 4,000 lb., the RTI-Military was 104 in. long, 64 in. wide and 60 in. high. Now back in civilian colors, this tractor originally was furnished in the always drab Army green. A 1952 Minneapolis-Moline brochure illustrates the various axle configurations available at that time, right. An unusual option was the extended right-hand axle for the Type U and Type E tractors.

4 Front End Types To Choose From

MINNEAPOLIS-MOLINE
MM
MODERN MACHINERY

Type U

Type S

Type N

Type E

Type U—is a universal tractor with the two front wheels together. By reversing the front wheels a maximum spacing of 13½ inches can be obtained. The famous Universal U is farm proven to give year-round service on drawbar, belt pulley, and power take-off. A complete line of mounted and pull-behind implements is available to fit your farm.

Type S—is one of the most powerful four-wheel standard tractors on the market. The extra weight resulting from heavy duty construction adds to the pulling power of the U. The rear wheel tread is set at 57 inches or 62½ inches and the front wheels at 50½ inches.

Type N—a universal tractor with a single front wheel designed for the farmer who needs an efficient, powerful, 3 plow tractor in narrow-row crops. This type is identical with type U except for the front wheel and a rear wheel tread of 96 inches.

Type E—Has a front axle permitting tread adjustment at intervals of 4 inches from 56 to 84 inches. This model combines all the features of the Standard with the versatility of the Universal. It can be used for work in narrow row crops as well as wide, because of the versatile tread adjustment. Steering arms are made of drop-forged steel for greatest possible strength. Rear tread 54½ to 88½ inches.

Long Right-Hand Axle for Types U and E

As optional equipment, a long right-hand axle is available to permit moving the wheel out to a 52-inch tread. This spacing permits harvesting of beets grown in 18-, 20-, or 22-inch rows. The left-hand axle is not changed.

Safe, smooth, and comfortable operation assured by adjustable seat, non-slip platform, and hand operated twin-disc clutch. Drawbar swing of 22 inches permits easier

Page Ten

The **Inside Sto**

1. Centrifugal water pump mounted on bronze bushings, gear-driven automatic water pump seal.

2. Large-capacity, 6-gallon tubular radiator.

3. V-belt driven fan mounted on Timken roller bearing.

4. Thermostat for control of water temperature.

5. Heavy-duty air cleaner.

6. Oil filter with easily replaceable waste-type cartridge.

7. Moss-type breather with extra capacity assures proper crankcase ventilation.

8. Fuel filter has a filter element made up of several per discs to remove foreign particles.

9. Seam-welded gas tank, 21-gallon capacity.

10. Modern instrument panel with ammeter, oil ga temperature gauge, light switch, fuse holder, sta and instrument light.

11. Wobble-stick gear shift—5 forward speeds and 1 verse speed: Low—2.7, 2nd—3.8, 3rd—4.4, 4t 6.4, 5th—14.8, reverse—2.1.

12. Four-pinion differential runs in a bath of oil. Revac type bevel gears.

13. New Flote-Ride seat features various adjustments the comfort of the operator and a shock absor utilizing both spring and fluid assembly.

ONOMICAL • DEPENDABLE

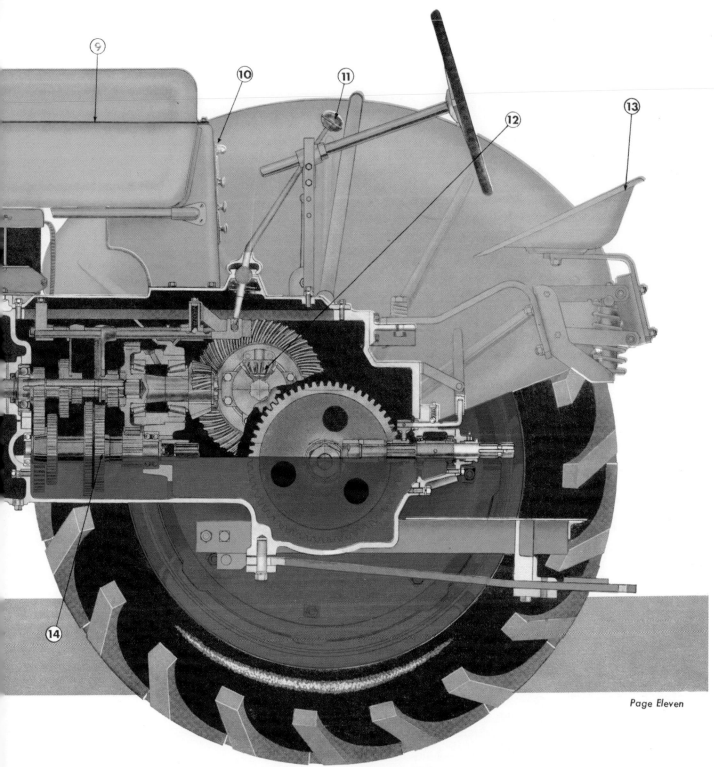

Page Eleven

Transmission shafts and gears are made of special alloy steel mounted on tapered roller and ball bearings. Transmission runs in a bath of oil.

Transmission is sealed against dust and dirt by felt seals.

Heavy-duty, over-center, twin-disc clutch, which is hand operated.

Replaceable crankshaft, main and connecting bearings are precision made of steel lined with babbitt.

18. Force-feed filter lubrication to connecting rods and main bearings, valve mechanism, camshaft, accessory shaft, timing gears, and governor.

19. Oil pump with extra capacity for positive lubrication.

20. Heavy-duty precision-made cast iron piston with 3 compression rings and 1 oil ring.

21. Distributor specifically designed for farm use, sealed against dust, dirt, with a greater resistance to entrance of moisture.

22. Worm and hardened sector steering gear mounted on roller bearings, runs in bath of oil.

87

This Minneapolis-Moline Model G was photographed at the Mid-Iowa Antique Power Association Show, Marshalltown, Iowa, in 1989. The GT engine, with its 4⅝ x 6 in. bore and stroke, was designed just prior to World War II. For M-M and other tractor builders, the outbreak of war virtually shelved farm tractor production and greatly slowed the development of new engines and new tractor models.

FACTORY BUILT
another MM FIRST

LP GAS
since 1941
U

Cheaper by the Hour...10% More Power...
Safety Engineered...Longer Engine Life

Minneapolis-Moline has been building the LP gas Model U since 1941. This long experience has shown that certain changes are necessary in tractor design to obtain the best performance from LP gas.

HEAVY-DUTY DESIGN—Large bearing surfaces and extra strength of all parts to withstand high compression power.

HIGH-COMPRESSION EFFICIENCY—MM Model U LP gas tractor is built with special high compression heads, designed for high turbulence and maximum efficiency with LP gas.

REGULATED COOLING—Large cooling water jackets with directed flow to hottest parts around the combustion chamber provide adequate cooling for best performance. Thermostat control maintains uniform temperatures and volume water circulation.

Minneapolis-Moline proudly pointed to its achievement of being the first company to offer a factory-built LP-gas tractor to the farming public. This was way back in 1941! The illustration dates to 1952.

For 1955 the Universal ZB tractor listed at $1,840, above, but the optional LP-gas equipment as shown on this model added another $206 to the list price. Minneapolis-Moline pioneered the use of LP-gas as a tractor fuel. M-M engines for this fuel were regularly equipped with a 12 volt electrical system for better ignition performance. Also featured were stellite valve seats for long and troublefree operation. From this view you can see that the gas storage tank slightly obstructed the view when compared to standard gasoline models. Minneapolis-Moline quoted its ZB tractor as having a maximum output of 32 hp when equipped for LP-gas, on the next pages. The 206 ci, four-cylinder engine used a 3⅝ x 5 in. bore and stroke. Company advertising spoke of the high ratio of connecting-rod length to the cylinder bore, citing this feature as resulting in greater power and efficiency on LP-gas. The ZB tractors were available in the standard tricycle style, single front wheel and wide, adjustable-front-axle types.

UB Special Diesel Model with new interchangeable front-end assemblies and exclusive MM power steering system.

An interesting variation of the Model U series is this UTC Cane tractor of 1948, above. Designed specifically for the demands of this crop, the UTC offered the exceptionally high clearance required for this service. Minneapolis-Moline offered this model from 1948 through 1954. Although Minneapolis-Moline had pioneered the use of LP-gas fuel for farm tractors, left, M-M engineers were more cautious in adopting diesel engines as optional or standard equipment. By the early 1950s the company had decided on the Lanova combustion system. Originally developed by Franz Lang, the Lanova system had been successfully used on numerous truck and tractor engines

with excellent success. New developments in diesel engine design soon led to the abandonment of the Lanova system in favor of improved designs. The M-M UB Special Diesel model was marketed in the mid 1950s. It featured new interchangeable front-end assemblies and the exclusive M-M power steering system. The diesel engine was of four-cylinder design with a displacement of 283 ci. A front-end view of the UTC Cane tractor, right, illustrates the high-arch front axle which was a primary feature of this model. The UTC was originally introduced in 1943 as the Model U Cane tractor and carried the same general specifications as the UTS

models. Standard equipment included a gasoline engine, but fenders and belt pulley were not part of the package.

This unique Model UTC Cane tractor of 1948 is owned by Leroy Wonder of Danbury, Iowa. Like the regular Model U series, it featured a four-cylinder engine having a 4¼ x 5 in. bore and stroke with an overhead-valve design. For 1954 this model had a suggested retail price of $3,200.

Minneapolis-Moline Power Implement Company 1950–1969

Farming in the Modern Age

The letter series tractors continued into the 1950s, and included numerous innovations and additions in keeping with the rapid advances in farm tractor design. By the mid 1950s features such as power steering, full hydraulics and many other conveniences were optionally available if not included as standard equipment. Closing out the letter series tractors was the G-VI model. This tractor was in the

In the 50 hp class, the Five Star tractor was built from 1957 to 1961. Features included Ampli-Torc, a trade name for the power booster system. Built-in power steering was standard equipment, as were the three-point hitch and an independent PTO. Power-adjusted rear wheels took the hard work out of this task, and three different front ends were available— the standard tricycle style, single front wheel or an extendible wide front axle. This radiator view displays a modern M-M trademark design.

70 hp class and could be furnished with the choice of a diesel or an LP-gas engine. In 1964 it carried a list price of $6,400.

The Motrac crawler tractor was built in 1960–61. This model was equipped with a 206 ci engine, of either gas or diesel design. The engine was of four-cylinder design, using a 3⅝ x 5 in. bore and stroke. It weighed approximately 9,300 lb. From all available information, production of the Motrac was quite limited.

The Jet Star tractors were featured from 1959–62, followed in 1963 with the Jet Star 2, and the Jet Star 3 in 1964–70. The Four Star series was produced from 1959–62, and the Five Star models were built from 1957–61. The M-5 was offered in 1960–63, while the U-302 series was built in the 1964–70 period.

During 1956 the 335 tractor was introduced. Production ceased in 1961. A 445 model was built in the 1956–59 period.

The last of the M series tractors made their debut in 1962 with the M-504. It was closed out the following year. Then in 1963 came the M-602 and M-604 models—they both ended in 1964. Following these tractors came the M-670 in 1964, and it remained until 1970.

The G series tractors included: the G-704 of 1962; G-705 of 1962–65; G-706 of 1962–65; G-707 and G-708 of 1965; G-900 of 1967–69; G-950 of 1969–71; G-955 of 1973; G-1000 of 1965–69; G-1000 Vista of 1967–69; G-1050 and G-1350 of 1969–71; and G-1355 of 1972–73.

Other tractor models included the four-wheel-drive tractors with the A4T designation. These models were also sold under Oliver and White model designators. The two four-wheel-drive models were the A4T-1400 for 1969–70 and the A4T-1600 for 1970–72. Also of significance is the Uni-Tractor, built by M-M in 1951–62.

Minneapolis-Moline bought out the B. F. Avery line in 1951. Avery production included: Avery A of 1945-50; Avery V of 1946-52; Avery BF of 1950-53 and the (M-M) BG of 1953-55.

No information has been located on the Big Mo tractors built in the 1959-66 period.

Of lesser significance is the Town & Country series offered from 1969 to 1972. These lawn and garden tractors consisted of the 107, 109, 110, 112 and 114 models, the last two digits indicating the horsepower of the tractor. The 10, 12 and 14 hp sizes were optionally available with a hydrostatic drive.

The final merger

After forty years of successful innovations in the farm equipment industry, in 1969 Minneapolis-Moline lost its identity through a merger. In that year M-M joined with Oliver Farm Equipment Corp. and the Cockshutt Farm Equipment Co. of Canada to form White Farm Equipment Co. with headquarters in Oak Brook, Illinois. The new company was a division of White Motor Company of Cleveland, Ohio.

Once again, a rapidly changing industry had brought these companies full circle. Minneapolis-Moline was organized in 1929, primarily as a means of staying in the farm equipment business. The

Built in the 1949–53 period, M-M's ZAS tractor carried the same general specifications as the ZAU except that the ZAS offered fixed front and rear treads. A belt pulley was optionally available for $34 over the standard list price of $2,000. Like many other models of this period, it could also be equipped for LP-gas, either as a factory-installed option or for field installation. This 1951 model from the Roger Mohr Collection displays the new-style square radiator and small wings.

In about 1954, Minneapolis-Moline announced diesel-powered tractors in addition to its gasoline-powered models. Initially, these engines were designed around the Lanova system of fuel injection and combustion. The Lanova design used an energy cell directly opposite the injector. This was the major principle of Lanova's Controlled Turbulence combustion. Early offerings included the U and UB diesels, along with the huge Model G diesel tractor. This model carried a 1955 list price of $4,320. Standard features included a six-cylinder engine with a 4¼ x 5 in. bore and stroke and a rated speed of 1300 rpm. The GBD weighed in at 7,400 lb.

revolutionary changes to power farming had forced the three participants to join forces as a means to an end. Oliver Farm Equipment had experienced virtually the same thing at about the same time. The tremendous upheaval of change in farming practices once again forced the individual firms to either liquidate plants and equipment or pursue the more painful course of attrition: being literally chewed to pieces by their competitors. The only viable alternative seemed to be a merger whereby the individual

firms could pool their resources, thus maintaining an important position in the industry. Since the 1969 merger which formed White Farm Equipment, agriculture has seen still more changes. Who can guess the state of the industry in another generation.

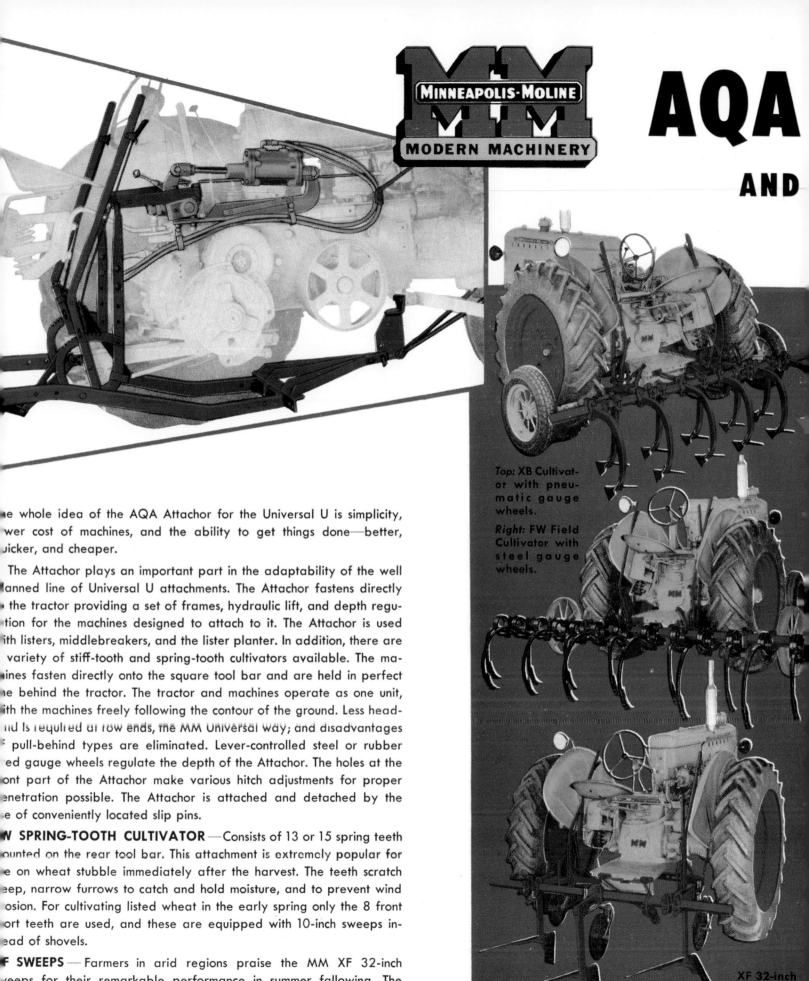

Top: XB Cultivator with pneumatic gauge wheels.

Right: FW Field Cultivator with steel gauge wheels.

XF 32-inch sweeps.

...e whole idea of the AQA Attachor for the Universal U is simplicity, ...wer cost of machines, and the ability to get things done—better, ...uicker, and cheaper.

The Attachor plays an important part in the adaptability of the well ...lanned line of Universal U attachments. The Attachor fastens directly ... the tractor providing a set of frames, hydraulic lift, and depth regu-...tion for the machines designed to attach to it. The Attachor is used ...ith listers, middlebreakers, and the lister planter. In addition, there are ... variety of stiff-tooth and spring-tooth cultivators available. The ma-...ines fasten directly onto the square tool bar and are held in perfect ...ne behind the tractor. The tractor and machines operate as one unit, ...ith the machines freely following the contour of the ground. Less head-...nd is required at row ends, the MM Universal way; and disadvantages ... pull-behind types are eliminated. Lever-controlled steel or rubber ...ed gauge wheels regulate the depth of the Attachor. The holes at the ...ont part of the Attachor make various hitch adjustments for proper ...enetration possible. The Attachor is attached and detached by the ...e of conveniently located slip pins.

...W SPRING-TOOTH CULTIVATOR—Consists of 13 or 15 spring teeth ...ounted on the rear tool bar. This attachment is extremely popular for ...e on wheat stubble immediately after the harvest. The teeth scratch ...eep, narrow furrows to catch and hold moisture, and to prevent wind ...osion. For cultivating listed wheat in the early spring only the 8 front ...ort teeth are used, and these are equipped with 10-inch sweeps in-...ead of shovels.

... SWEEPS—Farmers in arid regions praise the MM XF 32-inch ...veeps for their remarkable performance in summer fallowing. The ...veeps cut the weeds below the surface leaving the stubble and weeds

Introduced in 1951 as the Model BF, right, this little tractor had originally been produced by B. F. Avery & Co., Louisville, Kentucky, back in 1945. Minneapolis-Moline took over Avery in 1951 and continued to build derivations of this small tractor into 1955. This particular model plays a curious role in the constant merger and takeover game. Originally, Avery built a small tractor for Cleveland Tractor Company. Oliver Corporation bought out Cleveland in 1944, and they in turn were purchased by White Motors in 1960. White then purchased Minneapolis-Moline in 1969. This rather rare tractor is part of the Roger Mohr Collection. Although the 1952 Minneapolis-Moline tractors were not furnished with a three-point system, on the previous page, company engineers responded with their own AQA Attachor as a means of quickly changing from one implement to another.

From 1956 to 1961 Minneapolis-Moline offered its Power Line series with Ampli-Torc, on the previous pages. This was the M-M trade name for a torque amplifier system that consisted of a planetary drive between the clutch and the gearbox. Operated by hydraulics, the Ampli-Torc system gave the equivalent of 10 forward speeds from a five-speed gearbox. This gave somewhat of an overlap to the gear selection and permitted speed control unlike anything previously offered. The three-point lift system was in keeping with industry trends. This 1957 Model 335 Utility is a part of the Roger Mohr Collection. With about 35 belt hp, right, the Model 335 featured the four-cylinder, 3⅝ x 4 in. engine similar to that which was used for some years previous. Available either in the tricycle or in a utility design, the 335 remained in production through 1961. For that year it retailed at $2,498. The Ampli-Torc option added another $148, power steering added $110 and a front PTO drive was available for an additional $43.

In 1957 Minneapolis-Moline replaced the Model UB with an entirely new Five Star series, on the previous pages. Available for use with gasoline, LP-gas or tractor fuel, the Five Star could also be furnished in a diesel-equipped version. Curiously, however, the gasoline-powered model was not tested at Nebraska—only the LP-gas version appears under Test Number 651, and the diesel-powered model immediately after with Test Number 652. Both of these tests were made in 1958. Often nicknamed the Minneapolis-Moline Motorcycle, above, the M-M Uni-Harvestor was announced by the company in January 1951. Developed by Martin Ronning, chief engineer of the farm machinery division, it was intended as the chassis and power unit for an entire series of self-propelled farm machines. Ronning conceived the Uni-Harvestor idea in 1945, but progress was stymied because of World War II and the early postwar years. The original Uni-Tractor was equipped with a V-type four-cylinder engine built by Minneapolis-Moline. It used a 3⅝ x 5

in. bore and stroke. For 1955, the base unit was priced at $2,790. This example is owned by Vernon Parizek of Elberon, Iowa.

Another view of the Uni-Tractor illustrates the simplicity of the bare machine. Initially, M-M offered its Uni-Foragor (forage harvester), Uni-Harvestor (combine) and Uni-Picker (corn picker) attachments. To these were added numerous other attachments, including the Uni-Baler (hay baler). By the mid 1960s the base price of the Uni-Tractor had risen to $3,895.

Production of the Minneapolis-Moline Four Star series ran from 1959 to 1964, left. This 1961 model is part of the Roger Mohr Collection. At the Nebraska Tractor Test Laboratory in Lincoln, the Four Star demonstrated 44.57 PTO hp using gasoline fuel and 45.54 PTO hp with LP-gas. The test results are contained in Test Numbers 789 and 790. Always designed with an eye toward easy maintenance, the modern engine featured Moline's exclusive removable cylinder blocks and a rigid, single-unit crankcase and basepan construction. The cylinders were cast in pairs for easy service.

Minneapolis-Moline offered the Four Star in a regular design as well as the Four Star Super, above. The latter style was virtually identical, except that modern features such as a comfortable upholstered seat, deluxe nonglare instrument panel and power adjustable rear wheels came as standard equipment. For 1964 this tractor carried a list price of $3,298. A Four Star diesel-equipped model was offered from 1962 to 1964. It listed at slightly over $3,900. This G706 LP-gas model, on the next pages, is owned by Dick Allen of Newton, Iowa. Bearing serial number 23600660, it carries the same series of numbers as Massey-Ferguson's MF–97 model, and in fact, the latter was built by Minneapolis-Moline for Massey-Ferguson. Actually, the arrangement began in 1958 when Massey-Ferguson bought what was basically the M-M GBD and Gvi tractors and changed some sheet metal, the paint and the decals, with the result being the Massey-Ferguson 95. The G706 was produced from 1963 to 1967.

A view from the operator's platform illustrates the method of nestling the LP-gas fuel tank within the hood of the G706 tractor. Minneapolis-Moline originally rated the G705 and G706 tractors at 105 flywheel hp, but raised this figure to an output of 112 hp. The LP-gas version used a big six-cylinder engine with a 4⅝ x 5 in. bore and stroke for a displacement of 504 ci. The G705 was a standard two-wheel-drive model, and the G706 was of four-wheel-drive design.

The G706 Diesel was tested at Nebraska in 1963 under Test Number 833. The test weight for this unit was 9,165 lb. This test indicated a maximum of 102 PTO hp. Produced in the 1962–65 period, the G705 and G706 tractors were the largest of the M-M line. Some of the dealer guides indicate that these models may have been available as late as 1967. For 1965, however, the G705 Diesel was priced at $6,725 and the G706 listed at $8,725.

The U–302 tractors are listed in a gasoline version from 1964 to 1972, and in a diesel model for the 1967–72 period. This advertisement is from 1965.

Minneapolis-Moline built only 429 of the MF–97 tractors for Massey-Ferguson. They were available with the choice of gasoline, diesel or, as in this example, LP-gas fuel. The Model 97 was built over the G705, 706, 707 or 708 chassis. The G705 and G707 were two-wheel-drive models, with the latter being simply an updated version of the former number. The G706 and G708 tractors were equipped with power-assist front wheels, and the G708 was a new version of the earlier G706. This example is owned by Martha Stochl of Toledo, Iowa.

From the Roger Mohr Collection comes this attractively restored G706 tractor of 1964 vintage. This particular tractor is equipped with a factory-installed three-point hitch, making it rather unique. When first announced in late 1962, the standard equipment included a five-speed gearbox, deluxe upholstered seat, full instrumentation and full crown fenders. Options included a belt pulley, power takeoff shaft, rice tires and wheel weights.

A view of the big 504 ci engine of the G706 tractor shows its tremendous size. Throughout their career, M-M engineers promoted the advantages of the long-stroke engine. Looking at the engine as the very heart of the tractor, they cited the long stroke and low operating speed as conducive to extra lugging power and long engine life.

A view of the operator's platform on the G706 provides some perspective on the size of this tractor. Measuring 150½ in. in length, it is 84½ in. wide and stands at 82 in. high. The rear wheel tread measures 8 ft.

Produced in the 1960–64 period, the M5 tractors featured a four-cylinder engine of 336 ci displacement and a 4⅝ x 5 in. bore and stroke, on the previous pages. For 1964 the gasoline model listed at $4,812. The Ampli-Torc planetary system gave 10 forward speeds from a five-speed gearbox, and power steering was standard equipment. The hood and grille design typify the company's trend toward new and more modern tractors. At a time when at least a portion of the competing manufacturers were opting

for smaller, high-speed engines with square or over-square bore and stroke ratios, Minneapolis-Moline opted for a continuation of the slower speed and longer stroke engines as being the best approach to maximum lugging power and long engine life. This tractor is in the Roger Mohr Collection. Built at the Hopkins, Minnesota, plant of White Industries, the M-M A4T tractor was marketed between 1969 and 1971, above. This same tractor was also sold in 1971 as the Oliver 2655 and as the White Plainsman in 1970. In 1970 it

was also offered as a special American Heritage version in red, white and blue with stars to commemorate the American Bicentennial Celebration of 1976.

A 1971 advertisement illustrates the G1350 White M-M tractor, above. It was also marketed as the Oliver 2155 model. Available with the choice of a diesel or an LP-gas engine, this model delivered approximately 155 PTO hp. Although this tractor is shown in American Heritage color patterns, the standard production models were finished in yellow with white and black trim. Coming to the late 1980s, on the next pages, this White American 60 was the latest of the American series tractors from White-New Idea. These are the first tractors of under 90 hp to be built within the United States for a decade.

Index